ELLE

PARIS

ELLE
PARIS

FOLLOW THE GUIDE !
THE CITY'S 450 BEST SPOTS

by **Camille Girette** and **Sabine Roche**
Illustrations: **Soledad**

CHÊNE

FOREWORD

ELLE is not only Parisian, it is French — and it loves to travel the world.

ELLE was born in Paris, this is where its heart lies, its loves bud,
its adventures take place — and ELLE loves its city so much, it knows
it like the back of its hand. Even so, the promise of finding a brand-new
place at the corner of a street gives ELLE a thrilling pleasure.

Dearest readers, these are Parisian spots chosen by ELLE.
Some are confidential, some are well-known, some are iconic and some
opened only recently. These are our "real" places: places we go
to — we swear it — and places we truly love.

Follow Camille and Sabine. With Soledad, they will open all the doors
for you!

Françoise-Marie SANTUCCI,
Editor-in-Chief

EDITORIAL

Our job is to explore Paris. To open doors, look for gems, discover new places, new trends and know-hows.... and to share them with our readers, week after week.

For years, we have witnessed perpetual changes in Paris. This felt like a good time to gather all our great spots in a guidebook.

The idea seemed simple, but going through with it was not that easy: How to choose? We all agreed that this ELLE best-of should not be a soulless inventory, but a subjective list of all our personal favorites and of the small, sometimes unknown stores that make Paris what it is. Hopefully, these 450 places will make you want to walk through the city to look for more.

We have also invited about twenty "friends of ELLE" to tell us about their secret and essential spots: stylists, bakers, chefs, designers – these people make Paris a moveable feast.

Now, all you have to do is follow the guide!

Camille GIRETTE and **Sabine ROCHE,**
Journalists at ELLE Paris

The phone numbers in this book are for making calls when in France. If you want to call from outside the country, dial your country's code to make an international call, followed by 33 to call into France, then dial the phone, but drop the 0 at the front so you use only nine digits.

CONTENTS

FASHION

PARIS, CAPITAL OF THE FASHION WORLD
SINCE THE BEGINNINGS OF FASHION

CHIC
BOUTIQUES
THE BEST MULTIBRAND STORES
TO SHOP FOR YOUR HAPPINESS

SOWEARE
YOUNG DESIGNERS
This shop window has a stunning design, a super-trendy mood board that changes each month, displaying a selection of the young and bright names of the fashion world, accessory designers, small decorative objects and gadgets at affordable prices. A gold mine!
40, rue de Charonne (11ᵗʰ). M° Ledru-Rollin, Bastille.
Phone: 09 82 37 63 91.
soweare-shop.fr

SoWeAre

LE66
THE GIANT ON
THE CHAMPS-ELYSĒES
Hidden in a mall, this place is a good find on the Champs-Elysées. What is its secret? 13,000 square feet with more than 150 brands, from average to high-end quality (Iro, Theory, etc.), an organic and vegetarian restaurant by Café Pinson, and a special counter to pick up online orders. One of the spaces has even been transformed into a drugstore that sells perfume, stationery, goodies, jewelry, and high tech gadgets, etc.
66, avenue des Champs-Ēlysées (8ᵗʰ).
M° Frankin D. Roosevelt, George V.
Phone: 01 53 53 33 80.
le66.fr

ROXAN
A CLEAR SELECTION
The Roxan is well established with two shops in Pigalle: the rue Lepic shop is all women's wear, and the rue des Martyrs shop is mixed. They offer a good selection of brands that we love – Notify, Masscob, Pomandère – along with smaller Nordic brands. This is one of the best places in the neighborhood to achieve a casual-chic look.
41, rue des Martyrs (9ᵗʰ). M° Saint-Georges, Notre-Dame-de-Lorette. Phone: 01 48 74 48 46.
25, rue Lepic (18ᵗʰ). M° Blanche, Abbesses.
Phone: 01 42 52 47 70.

ABOU D'ABI BAZAR
PERSONAL SHOPPING

This must-visit multibrand has been a safe bet for twenty years. It has four shops in the Marais and another, well-located shop, in the 5th arrondissement. You will find iconic items from new designers and well-established brands (Sha'Cha, AML, G.Kero). Overstretched working girls can plan personal shopping sessions after hours.

125, rue Vieille-du-Temple (3rd).
M° Saint-Séba stien-Froissart, Filles-du-Calvaire.
Phone: 01 42 71 13 26.
33, rue du Temple (4th). M° Hôtel-de-Ville, Rambuteau.
Phone: 01 44 61 37 24.
59, rue des Francs-Bourgeois (4th).
M° Hôtel-de-Ville, Rambuteau.
Phone: 01 40 33 24 59.
15, rue Soufflot (5th). RER Luxembourg,
M° Cluny-La Sorbonne. Phone: 01 42 77 96 98.
aboudabibazar.com

Abou d'Abi Bazar

TRY-ONS AT HOME

Igloo is an app that lets you try on clothes from around a hundred Parisian boutiques in your own home. You can order up to six items, which will be delivered within the next five hours by bike at a time of your choosing. The delivery person will pick up the items you do not want 24 hours later. This service is provided for only €1.
Available on the Apple App Store and Google Play.
igloo.paris

Simone

SIMONE
BOHEMIAN-CHIC
This place is the sweet fashion surprise
of the 7th arrondissement, right next to the Bon Marché. It is held by two fashionistas who skim through all the professional fairs to put together the trendiest bohemian-chic selection. Brands that are more or less known (Maison Père, Roses Roses, Nathalie Dumeix, etc.) create a mix-and-match style that is 100 percent ELLE-approved.
1, rue de Saint-Simon (7th). M° Rue du Bac, Solférino. Phone: 01 42 22 81 40.

By Marie

BY MARIE
DESIGNS AND JEWELS
Marie Gas fulfills all Parisian women's fashion desires with her first shop on rue Etienne Marcel, which celebrates a bohemian-chic style, and another on avenue George-V, where her luxurious selections perfectly mirror the surrounding neighborhood. Marie is also a designer. She displays some of her work in her shops, and under the family brand Gas Bijoux, which owns four other shops in Paris.
44, rue Étienne-Marcel (2nd). M° Les Halles, Sentier. Phone: 01 42 33 36 04.
8, avenue George-V (8th). M° Alma-Marceau, RER Pont de l'Alma. Phone: 01 53 23 88 00.
bymarie.fr

FrenchTrotters

Les Voltigeuses

ROYALCHEESE
CASUAL WEAR

This laid-back shrine has six locations
that carry a trendy and affordable selection
of women's clothing, with one shop offering
mixed clothing. Shoes and Vans sneakers
top off the perfect style.

22, rue Tiquetonne (2nd).
M° Étienne Marcel.
Phone: 09 50 16 42 75.
royalcheese.com

LES VOLTIGEUSES
ADORABLE AND AFFORDABLE

**What was Camille Lafond and Eugénie
Allez's wonderful idea?** To open a store that
mixes young designer items with affordable
brands (like Grace and Mila). They then
opened another store, a few blocks away,
entirely devoted to shoes, purses and jewelry.
All of this is happening in the upcoming
10th arrondissement, where new bars,
restaurants and trendy hotels open each day.
55, rue des Petites-Écuries (10th). M° Château d'Eau,
Bonne Nouvelle. Phone: 01 42 46 12 38.
45, rue des Petites-Écuries (10th). M° Château d'Eau,
Bonne Nouvelle. Phone: 09 83 45 59 76.
lesvoltigeuses.com

Kyrie Eleison

KYRIE ELEISON
RETRO VIBES
This is the place for chic, timeless and retro wardrobes – vintage dresses from British brands, pretty French needlework and shoes designed by the founder of the shop (starting at €150). Author signings are organized regularly to make the place even livelier.

15, carrefour de l'Odéon (6ʰ). M° Odéon.
Phone: 01 46 34 26 91.

BRAND BAZAR
PERSONAL ADVICE
Close to Le Bon Marché, this store is full of 12-to-90-year-old fans searching for the trendiest items of the season. Saleswomen with personal shopper energy offer advice on clothes, jewelry and accessories from about fifty different brands, spanning two floors.

33, rue de Sèvres (6ʰ).
M° Sèvres-Babylone.
Phone: 01 45 44 40 02.
brandbazar.com

VANESSA SEWARD
FASHION DESIGNER

HER SHOP:
CHARVET
"I just discovered a floor devoted to tailored shirts, with an incredible choice of poplin fabric, and another devoted to nighttime clothing that carries the most beautiful selection of pajamas and night robes I have ever seen."

28, place Vendôme (1ᵉʳ). M° Opéra.
Phone: 01 42 60 30 70.

Brand Bazar

Victoire

VICTOIRE
VARIED PLEASURES
This brand owns five Parisian stores:
three for women and two for men.
Representing the women's corner, each
location presents a slightly different selection:
very feminine in the 16th arrondissement,
slightly androgynous in the 6th, and in the
historic boutique on the Place des Victoires,
the art director mixes and matches personal
designs with current favorites.
10, rue du Colonel-Driant (1st).
M° Palais Royal-Musée du Louvre, Les Halles.
Phone: 01 47 03 05 88. (men)
10, place des Victoires (2nd). M° Sentier, Bourse.
Phone: 01 49 27 94 76. (women)
1, rue Madame (6th). M° Saint-Sulpice.
Phone: 01 45 49 23 94. (women)
15, rue du Vieux-Colombier (6th). M° Saint-Sulpice.
Phone: 01 42 22 40 96. (men)
16, rue de Passy (16th). M° Passy.
Phone: 01 46 47 90 70. (women)
monvictoire.fr

CENTRE COMMERCIAL
FAIR FASHION
In this concept store, Veja's founders display
the best items from fair trade and local
productions. You can shop there for classics,
stylish creations, beautiful footwear, but also
for ceramics, candles and books. And let's not
forget the many events that are hosted there.
2, rue de Marseille (10th).
M° Jacques Bonsergent, République.
Phone: 01 42 02 26 08.
centrecommercial.cc

Centre Commercial

HOME DRY CLEANING

Thanks to Washr, the website and the app, your clothes and linens can be dry-cleaned within 24 hours. This professional door-to-door service is available every day until 10 p.m. in Paris and nearby suburbs, with home pickup and drop-off for urgent and long-term planned requests.

washr.fr

AB33
SUCCESSFUL LOOKS

In this tiny shop, about thirty brands are chosen for their style, design and fabrics. You can follow trends on the website ab33.fr where the catalog of seasonal fashions is particularly well done. In the shop, children can keep busy drawing and playing with toys.

33, rue Charlot (3rd). M° Filles du Calvaire.
Phone: 01 42 71 02 82.
ab33.fr

SPREE
TOP OF THE RANGE

On entering, you will notice the designer furniture from the 1950's to the 80's bargains found by Bruno. Then, you will find high-end pieces, by designers who are not always well known, but who are all extremely talented and have been spotted by Roberta. This artsy place is across the street from the art gallery owned by the same couple.

16, rue La Vieuville (18th). M° Abbesses.
Phone: 01 42 23 41 40.
spree.fr

Spree

MARCELLE
MINI AND MAXI

This tiny boutique in South Pigalle gathers a wonderful selection of designers (G. Kero, Samsøe, My Sunday Morning) that you won't find anywhere else in the neighborhood, along with some men's clothes, candles and photographs by the Lola James Harper collective. They have already achieved a similar feat at Pignon-sur-rue (29, rue Truffaut, 17th), their first multibrand store in Batignolles.

30, rue Henri-Monnier (9th). M° Pigalle, Saint-Georges.
Phone: 01 71 27 39 62.
marcelle-marcelle.com

POLLEN
EXCELLENT SELECTION

Carole Sofia studied design, worked for a textile manufacturer, and opened a multibrand store. It is not so much the selection of brands in itself that makes this place different, but the intelligence with which they are put together. In this village-like area of the 19th arrondissement, clients rush to find the right Bellerose sweatshirt, a Diega long coat, or Caths' horn necklaces. Across the street, at number 6 in the shoe and accessories store, they look for THE right pair of boots, THE right blucher shoes or THE most beautiful scarf.

6, rue de la Villette (19th). M° Jourdain, Pyrénées.
Phone: 01 42 38 38 58.
7, rue de la Villette (19th). M° Jourdain, Pyrénées.
Phone: 01 42 02 31 20.

Pollen

Chéri

CHĒRI
NEW BRANDS

In her tiny boutique, Eloïse features young upcoming brands. Margaux Lonnberg jackets, Marieta Cox bags, Emilie Roche's Japanese pearl necklaces, Tricote moi un tattoo's sweatshirts or Atonis' Egyptian-inspired graphic bracelets. This is the perfect place for finding one-of-a-kind clothes and items to fill your closet.

8, rue Brochant (17th). M° Brochant.
Phone: 01 42 63 23 93.
boutiquecheri.tictail.fr

SOS DIRTY LAUNDRY

With the app and website Washapp, with just one click a "Washman" arrives at your door (home or office), starting at 8 a.m., to pick up clothes and linens. The clean laundry is returned within 48 hours and as late as 10 p.m. What makes Washapp different? It uses only eco-friendly products and packages.
washapp.fr

FASHION

SANDRA SERRAF
A SMOOTH SILHOUETTE

In the heart of Saint-Germain-des-Prés,
Sandra has been dressing elegant women for
twenty years. Her secret? A smooth silhouette
that combines a perfect cut with fine fabric.
Every season, she picks items from the
collections of Vanessa Bruno, Humanoid or
Laurence Bras, and she knows how to
introduce new designers like Xinera, made in
Los Angeles. And let's not forget her large
selection of jewels, bags, shoes and scarfs.
18, rue Mabillon (6th). M° Mabillon, Odéon.
Phone: 01 43 25 21 24.
sandraserraf.fr

THE BROKEN ARM
EXCLUSIVE DESIGNS

**Jacquemus, Carven, Christophe Lemaire,
Raf Simons** – each designer has a personal
rack. Anaïs Lafrange, Guillaume Steinmetz
and Romain Joste are crazy for top-of-the-line
clothes, complemented by a small selection of
accessories and sneakers, including exclusive
designs. The bonus is the outdoor terrace with
Wi-Fi, and the delightful cooking of chef
Linda Granebring.
12, rue Perrée (3rd).
M° Temple.
Phone: 01 44 61 53 60.
the-broken-arm.com

PAPERDOLLS
TALENT FINDER

**Looking like it came straight out of Alice in
Wonderland,** Paperdolls is a magical place
with chairs on the ceiling. Once the initial
surprise has passed, the hostess will invite you
to discover independent fashion designers and
young brands that produce locally and in small
series. Recently, the store started showcasing a
few bargain hunted items as well.
5, rue Houdon (18th). M° Pigalle.
Phone: 01 42 51 29 87.
paperdolls.fr

HELENE DARROZE
STARRED CHEF

HER MULTIBRAND
MONTAIGNE MARKET
"In this multibrand, Liliane Jossua offers
a beautiful designers' selection. I love
her boldness; I go there every time
I want to find a gift for a friend."
57, avenue Montaigne (8th).
M° Franklin D. Roosevelt.
Phone: 01 42 56 58 58.
montaignemarket.com

Les Petits Frenchies

L'EXCEPTION
THE FRENCH SPIRIT
**Located underneath the canopy in Les
Halles,** this boutique specializes in French
design, presenting the best of its selection in a
corner dedicated to a different designer every
ten days. It offers an area with seating for thirty,
where you can drink coffee all day or taste
delicious organic platters for lunch. Good
news: The showroom in the 10th arrondissement
has become an outlet store.
24, rue Berger (1st). RER Les Halles.
Phone: 01 44 61 90 26.
28, rue Bichat (10th). M° Goncourt.
lexception.com

L'Exception

LES PETITS FRENCHIES
A REAL-LIFE ONLINE BOUTIQUE

The concept? Finding new upcoming designers, showcasing them in articles on a web magazine and selling their items online. However, not everything happens on the Internet, and there is an actual showroom that opens for special and thematic sales, with fashion, accessories, jewelry, gastronomy and interior design events.

Watch this space!

15, passage du Bourg-l'Abbé (2nd).

M° Étienne Marcel, Réaumur-Sébastopol.

petitsfrenchies.com

N°2
VERY CHIC

This very chic multibrand store in the 7th has been dressing thirty-somethings and over for a few years. You will find off-the-rack designer items from Momoni of Italy, Hoss Intropia of Spain, Zenggi of Amsterdam and Gaëlle Barré, directly from her studio and boutique on rue Keller (11th). All of this forms a nice selection of cuts and fabrics. To top it all off, the team provides good advice.

2, rue Cler (7th). M° La Tour-Maubourg.

Phone: 01 45 50 11 54.

OWL Paris

RENT A DRESS

Nothing to wear for your job interview? For an important lunch or a networking cocktail party? No money to invest in a killer outfit? Rent one at *C'est Ma Robe*, a service that provides chic dresses and shockingly beautiful jackets.

1, rue des Prouvaires (1st).

M° Les Halles, Louvre-Rivoli.

Phone: 07 63 15 00 01.

cestmarobe.com

OWL PARIS
AFRICAN WAX PRINTS APLENTY

Julienne's personal creations mix wax with unicolor fabric. In her concept store, she gathers about thirty Afro-chic designers of women and men's clothing, as well as children's clothing, accessories, fine foods, plaids, cushions — it is a joyous mixed bag!

38, rue Caulaincourt (18th).

M° Blanche, Place de Clichy.

Phone: 01 77 10 76 84.

owlparis.com

ALL **SHOES**
SHOEMAKERS YOU SHOULD KNOW

ATELIER MERCADAL
ELEGANT AND COMFORTABLE

Marie-Laure Mercadal showcases her elegant and comfortable Italian-produced designs in a 1960's and 70's-inspired setting. The heels range from 0 to 4 3/4 inches. The star model is her pump that comes in five different heel heights. We just love the evening collection with golden soles. And her plan to open a second store on the right bank.
4, rue du Cherche-Midi (6ᵗʰ). M° Saint-Sulpice, Sèvres-Babylone. Phone: 01 40 33 02 43.
atelier-mercadal.com

Atelier Mercadal

L'ŒUF CHAUSSURES
GALLERY AND MULTIBRAND

The concept store called L'Œuf opened a gallery near Pigalle, as well as a multibrand shoe store. Foreign creations are featured, mostly flats, such as the Italian Gaia D'Este's very comfortable boots. This store is an asset for city dwellers in a hurry.
14, rue Clauzel (9ᵗʰ). M° Saint-Georges.
Phone: 01 73 73 86 82.
loeufparis.com

ANTHOLOGY PARIS
BOOTS AND BLUCHERS
AT A FAIR PRICE

Anthology is Anthony Knopfer's brand.
He already owns the store Roxan, as well as two beautiful multibrand stores in Pigalle. Anthology's shoes, mostly boots and bluchers, are made in Portugal and sold at a fair price. The item everyone is after is the Elvie shoelace-free blucher.
21, rue de Saintonge (3ʳᵈ). M° Filles du Calvaire, Saint-Sébastien Froissart. Phone: 01 42 78 11 34.
34, rue des Martyrs (9ᵗʰ). M° Saint-Georges.
Phone: 01 48 78 90 33. anthology-paris.com

Anthology Paris

Patricia Blanchet

PATRICIA BLANCHET
TWIST AND CHIC

Patricia Blanchet's shoes are often copied but never equaled, and they cause a commotion among stylish girls. Glitter trims, Art deco motifs, glitter lightning flashes on the side, incredible colors – her pumps and boots have a twist that makes all the difference. Come and see for yourself in this Parisian designer's unique boutique.

20, rue Beaurepaire (10th). M° Jacques Bonsergent, République. Phone: 01 42 02 35 85.
patriciablanchet.com

TILA MARCH
DETAIL-ORIENTED

Tamara Taichman is a fashion journalist for ELLE, but she is also known from Paris to Tokyo for her brand of bags and shoes. Her secret? We would say it is her innate attention to detail, such as shoes that are bi-fabric, bicolor, with bridle clasps or woven leather straps. You will find evidence of her sharp eye in all the collections she features each season in her Parisian boutiques.

19, place du Marché-Saint-Honoré (1st). M° Pyramides.
24, rue Saint-Sulpice (6th). M° Mabillon, Saint-Sulpice.
Phone: 01 43 26 69 20.
tilamarch.com

La Botte Gardiane

LA BOTTE GARDIANE
FRENCH TOUCH

More than 150 designs are featured, among them the famous boots from Camargo – a best seller. Boots, sandals, everything here is customizable and manufactured in France in the traditional way. Tailor-made shoes at a reasonable price.

25, rue du Bourg-Tibourg (4th).
M° Hôtel de Ville, Saint-Paul. Phone: 01 77 16 58 45.
25, rue de Charonne (11th). M° Ledru-Rollin, Bastille.
Phone: 09 51 11 05 15. 01 40 13 08 75.
labottegardiane.com

Tila March

POLDER
NORTHERN PIONEERS
A Northern wind blows on Polder.

Natalie Vodegel and Madelon Lanteri-Laura are Dutch designers, sisters, and pioneers of glitter socks, wooden-sole boots and trendy clogs. They give a very personal bohemian-chic style to their creations. Their bags, jewels and clothes are just as irresistible as their shoes.

13, rue des Quatre-Vents (6th).
M° Odéon, Mabillon.
Phone: 01 43 26 07 64.
polder.fr

Atelier Attal

ATELIER ATTAL
TAILOR-MADE GRACE
This is an outstanding shoemaker.

This artisan makes the sandal of your dreams to your size, or he can customize an existing item. During your first meeting with him, he will measure your feet and have you try on shoes to make sure the bridles are perfectly adjusted. As a finishing touch, your name will be engraved on the sole. Prices start at 150€ for women, 170€ for men and 90€ for children.

122, rue d'Assas (6th). RER Port-Royal,
M° Notre-Dame-des-Champs.
Phone: 01 46 34 52 33.

Polder

58M
SHARP CHOICES
This is THE reference in shoe multibrands.

We go there for the sharp selection of designers: Flamingos, Michel Vivien, Charlotte Olympia, Laurence Dacade... Designs are chic or rock, and sometimes created for this boutique exclusively.
A few jewels, scarfs, bags and clutches complete the selection.

58, rue Montmartre (2nd). M° Ētienne Marcel, Sentier.
Phone: 01 40 26 61 01.
58m.fr

FASHION

27 MILTON
ETHICAL PRODUCTION

This shop, divided into three, features Elodie Bruno's elegant shoes, Pairs in Paris' simple sneakers and Yvonne Yvonne's awesome leather or coated cloth bags. These three Parisian designers favor timeless designs, beautiful fabric and an ethical production process. Bravo to slow fashion!

27, rue Milton (9th). M° Saint-Georges.
elodiebruno.com
pairsinparis.fr
yvonneyvonne.fr

AVRIL GAU
TIMELESS FASHION

Avril Gau, who previously worked for Chanel and Clergerie, now excels as a bag and shoe designer and makes comfortable shoe designs with 2 to 3-inch heels. Her designs portray the timeless chic of classics and are produced in France and Portugal. We adore the attention to details that goes into the making of her bags and shoes, such as a glittered welt, a touch of color or a large brass clasp.

46, rue Croix-des-Petits-Champs (1st). M° Palais Royal-Musée du Louvre, Louvre-Rivoli. Phone: 01 42 61 21 60.
17, rue des Quatre-Vents (6th). M° Odéon, Mabillon.
Phone: 01 43 29 49 04.
avrilgau.com

SNEAKERSNSTUFF
COLLECTORS' CHOICE

Sneakersnstuff started off on the Internet. This welcoming loft with a Scandinavian feel is THE multibrand sneaker store, and it includes a large women's selection. Products from collaborations with major sneaker brands, such as Adidas, Puma and Vans, are also sold here.

95, rue Réaumur (2nd). M° Sentier.
Phone: 01 44 82 95 41.
sneakersnstuff.com

Sneakersnstuff

Avril Gau

ACCESSORIES
ARE KEY!

PRETTY SPOTS TO SHOP FOR WATCHES,
JEWELS, BAGS, GLASSES, ETC.

MARCH LA.B
RETRO WATCHMAKING

In the very select world of watchmaking, this new label sets itself apart by drawing inspiration from 1950's and 70's designs, and by producing entirely in France. Men's and women's collections are showcased in the Marais boutique with a 60's design, or in the small, confidential 70's styled gem underneath the arches of the Palais-Royal. Prices start at 475€.

83, galerie de Beaujolais (1ˢᵗ). M° Pyramides,
Palais Royal-Musée du Louvre. Phone: 01 45 08 03 62.
50, rue Charlot (3ʳᵈ). M° Filles du Calvaire,
Saint-Sébastien Froissart. Phone: 01 75 57 93 90.
march-lab.com

March LA.B

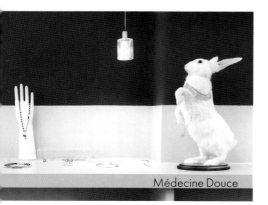

Médecine Douce

MÉDECINE DOUCE
A PRECIOUS REMEDY

The aerial skin jewelry designed by Marie Montaud is made with gold or gold plate, and it is sometimes ornamented with a stone, a thread or a shell. Long necklaces, bracelets, and cuffs are small remedies to everyday worries. Her "soft medicine," the translation of the name of her shop, operates perfectly.
10, rue de Marseille (10ᵗʰ).
M° Jacques Bonsergent, République.
Phone: 01 82 83 11 53.
bijouxmedecinedouce.com

CASOAR
TRADITIONAL JEWELRY

Charles Casoar, the designer and name behind this brand, makes traditional jewelry. His creations are modern-day interpretations of Baroque and Art deco styles. Traditional earrings, cameo rings, long earrings, you can be sure that your favorite jewel won't be worn by anyone else.

15, rue Boissy-d'Anglas (8th).
M° Madeleine, Concorde.
Phone: 01 47 42 69 51.

SOS ALTERATIONS AND SHOE REPAIR

Dry cleaning, alterations, shoe repair – SoyezBCBG picks up your defective items in 20 minutes from 6:50 a.m. to 8:50 a.m. or from 7 p.m. to 11 p.m. Your item is returned, as good as new and without an extra charge for delivery, within 48 hours.
soyezbcbg.fr

VERBREUIL PARIS
HIGH-END LEATHER CRAFT

This boutique is right next to the Luxembourg gardens and it looks just like an art gallery. Here, the artwork is composed of handmade, exotic leather bags, entirely produced in France. This new top-of-the-line leather craft brand focuses on minimalistic and modern designs with a customizable handle, and magnet or zipper openings.

4, rue de Fleurus (6th).
M° Rennes, Saint-Placide.
Phone: 01 45 49 22 69.
verbreuil.com

Verbreuil Paris

BIRDY
YOUNG FRENCH DESIGNERS

Birdy gathers all of the young jewelry designers we love in two stores: 5 Octobre, Pascale Monvoisin, Marie-Laure Chamorel – and the lesser-known Sharing, whose necklaces are composed of stones and thread woven by Tibetan nuns.

5, rue des Lombards (4th). M° Châtelet, Hôtel de Ville.
Phone: 09 73 18 68 68.
12, rue Saint-Placide (6th). M° Sèvres-Babylone, Vaneau.
Phone: 01 42 22 88 37. birdyboutique.fr

Atelier Couronnes

ATELIER COURONNES
JUST FOR YOU

In their beautiful studio-store,
Louise Damas shows her jewels with ornate settings, and Claire Rischette presents made-to-order bags by Fauvette Paris. A few other favorite products are featured in this store, where creative workshops are regularly organized by other artisans.

6, rue du Château-d'Eau (10th).
M° Jacques Bonsergent, République.
Phone: 01 40 37 03 54.
fauvette-paris.com
louisedamas.fr

BABY BUDDHA
THE BIG MIX

The mix-and-match bohemian style is apparent in this multibrand accessories store, which specializes in jewels. Delphine Delafon's bucket bags have been on the shelves since the beginning, next to Claris Virot's saddlebags. Craft jewels are also displayed, by color or style.

68, rue des Saints-Pères (7th). M° Sèvres-Babylone,
Saint-Germain-des-Prés. Phone: 01 45 48 08 00.
baby-buddha.com

E-CONCIERGE

Dry cleaning, laundry, ironing, alterations, shoe repair, copying keys – Quatre Epingles' website and app offers many services from different drop-off and pick-up locations around Paris. They will take care of whatever you need taken care of within 48 hours, working with local artisans.

quatreepingles.fr

MILAN LUNETIER
RARE DESIGNS

This is the place to go to adorn your or your child's face with designer sunglasses or prescription glasses. Milan finds designs abroad in every style that you will not see anywhere else: retro-chic, super feminine, technical. In this vast and welcoming boutique, you can take time to find the right pair for you. We love the very chic glasses chain necklace designed by Diffuser Tokyo.

27, rue de Charonne (11th).
M° Ledru-Rollin, Bastille.
Phone: 01 72 10 31 65.

Milan Lunetier

Le Sept Cinq

LE SEPT CINQ
JOYFULLY CREATIVE

In South Pigalle and underneath the canopy at Les Halles, these boutiques joyfully gather fashion and home design accessories from only Parisian creators (Royalties, Bobbies, Exquises Indécises, etc.). As a bonus, you can get sweet and savory treats in the tea shop at Les Halles, or even a full lunch.

26, rue Berger (1st). M° and RER Les Halles.
Phone: 09 83 00 44 01.
54, rue Notre-Dame-de-Lorette (9th).
M° Saint-Georges, Pigalle.
Phone: 09 83 55 05 95.
sept-cinq.com

HOD
AFFORDABLE JEWELRY

Valerie started studying to become a pharmacist, but after having discovered many designers in India and the trendy jewelry stores of LA and New York, she ended up working in jewelry.
Her boutique is an ode to refinement.
Her obsession is to make jewelry affordable – hence the lovely little home designs featured here at awesome prices!

104, rue Vieille-du-Temple (3rd).
M° Saint-Sébastien Froissart, Filles du Calvaire.
Phone: 09 53 15 83 34.
hod-boutique.com

Hod

White Bird

WHITE BIRD
WELCOMING GEMS

After working for jewelers on place Vendôme, Stéphanie Roger founded White Bird, two welcoming gems where each designer has a small window display. Among others, Cathy Waterman, Pippa Small and Dorette are featured.

38, rue du Mont-Thabor (1ᵉʳ). M° Concorde. Phone: 01 58 62 25 86.
7, boulevard des Filles-du-Calvaire (3ʳᵈ). M° Saint-Sébastien Froissart. Phone: 01 40 24 27 17.
whitebirdjewellery.com

IODĒ
RECYCLED GOLD AND SILVER

In this small setting, Virginie features delicate jewelry made on the spot in her studio from recycled gold and silver. She also shows some of her favorite items from brands that she loves, such as Trois Petits Points, Scosha or Les Poinçonneurs de Paris.

73, place du Docteur-Félix-Lobligeois (17ᵗʰ). M° Rome, Brochant.
Phone: 01 46 27 59 97.
iode-atelier.com

A PRO IN YOUR CLOSET

Pick out clothes, throw some out, recycle them, sell them – and finally adapt your wardrobe to your personality. You can actually get this done without paying too much. Anne-Marie Lecordier is a life coach that will help you through all of this with great talent and infinite kindness. The service she provides is indispensable if you want a perfect look but do not have time to tidy your closet or shop by yourself.
lecordier.com

Claire Naa

Mad Lords

Territori

MAD LORDS
CONFIDENTIAL AND CONCEPT
This somewhat secret and hidden concept store spans more than 2,000 square feet in a backyard. It is a great surprise: It presents a wide selection of jewels, especially for men, with an exclusive corner dedicated to Californian designer Maor Cohen. Check out this secret place for all of the great designers it features, and the tailor-made jewels you can order there.

316, rue Saint-Honoré (1st). M° Tuileries, Pyramides.
Phone: 01 45 25 08 31.
madlords.com

CLAIRE NAA
BRAILLE JEWELRY
Claire used to be a home design journalist before she started creating jewels you would not find anywhere else. Her collections in braille and origami are inspired. In her stores, plenty of other surprises await you: semiprecious stone necklaces by Caterina, silver and diamond rings by Diamanti Per Tutti, pearl and fabric necklaces by Marie-Laure Chamorel, etc.

45, rue de Turenne (3rd). M° Chemin Vert, Saint-Paul.
Phone: 01 42 71 77 52.
9, rue Saint-Sulpice (6th). M° Odéon, Mabillon.
Phone: 01 43 54 89 82. claire-naa.com

TERRITORI
UNIQUE DESIGNS
Territori is an invitation to travel, and the name of Alessandra Bruni's designer label. We love her pivotal rings and the necklaces that mix links and rough diamonds. Her jewels are one of a kind that she makes from objects or old jewels. Alessandra also shows works of other designers in her store: Les Yeux d'Elsa, Nini Peony, etc.

86, rue de Charonne (11th). M° Charonne.
Phone: 01 43 70 85 56.
territori-paris.com

DANTE & MARIA
SMALL SERIES

In a store that looks like a cabinet of curiosities, Agnès Sinelle, aka Dante & Maria, imagines unique pieces and items in small series. Necklaces, pendants made from shells dipped in fine gold, engraved rough medallions, mounted rings, aerial earrings — Dante & Maria's jewels in silver or gold plate have irresistible charm. As a bonus, the service is almost tailor-made and the prices are good.
3, rue de la Grange-aux-Belles (10th). M° République, Jacques Bonsergent. Phone: 01 70 22 62 13.
dantemaria.fr

5 OCTOBRE
STUDIO MEETING

We all know 5 Octobre's jewels, sold in multibrand stores, but few of us know that its creator, Sophie Pfeffer, has opened a studio-boutique in an old clockmaker's studio. It is open to the public on only a few Saturday afternoons a month (check the website for opening dates). It is the perfect setting to discover her poetic and refined collection.
3, rue Beautreillis (4th).
M° Sully-Morland, Bastille.
5octobre.com

Dante & Maria

Aime

AIME
ART DECO VIBE

Magali Pont, a prolific creator who is passionate about the 1920's and 30's, likes to reinterpret these styles in her work. Alongside a collection created for Vanessa Bruno, her Art Deco pieces are displayed in the showroom. We particularly love the way she handles matt gold in her necklaces and cuffs.
14, rue de Beauregard (2nd). M° Bonne Nouvelle.
aime-bijoux.fr

La Tonkinoise à Paris

LA TONKINOISE Ā PARIS
NEW OLD

Chantal Manoukian's designs are unique pieces that she makes from old jewels in her studio-boutique. The poetic necklaces that she calls "small worlds," the cuffs she makes from old watch bracelets and broaches, and the long necklaces that mix glass beads with rosary beads all illustrate the way she wonderfully mixes different styles.

80, rue Jean-Pierre-Timbaud (11th). M° Parmentier, Couronnes. latonkinoiseaparis.com.

IMAÏ
STRONG PIECES

Julie Borgeaud used to be a home design journalist, and now she designs jewelry. She excels at creating strong pieces that complete an outfit. Her graphic cuffs, big stone necklaces, heavy pendants are all shown in small series in her Parisian studio. As a bonus, prices are affordable and she provides a customization service to change a stone or shorten a chain.

1, rue Saint-Benoît (6th). M° Saint-Germain-des-Prés.
Phone: 01 42 03 70 08.
imai.fr.

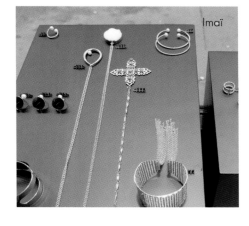

Imaï

MONSIEUR
VERY FEMININE

Behind "Monsieur," you will find the woman designer Nadia Azoug, who learned her new job as a jeweler late in life. There is nothing masculine about her brand – in fact, quite the contrary! We love her simple and refined style, particularly her wedding rings. Her custom-made work is done right in front of the client.

53, rue Charlot (3rd).
M° Filles du Calvaire, Temple.
Phone: 01 42 71 12 65.
monsieur-paris.com

Monsieur

Delphine Pariente

DELPHINE PARIENTE
A NICE STORY

In the Marais, Delphine has opened three shops with skillfully composed vintage decorations, creating a nice story. Her jewelry is displayed at number 19 on rue de Turenne. At number 101, you will find a studio to assemble necklaces yourselves. Unique pieces are made from old jewels and shown in the biggest of the three boutiques, found at number 10 on the rue des Filles-du-Calvaire. At Delphine Pariente's, everything is customizable, including the message you want to get through.

10, rue des Filles-du-Calvaire (3rd). M° Filles du Calvaire.
Phone: 01 44 61 16 21.
101, rue de Turenne (3rd). M° Filles du Calvaire.
Phone: 01 42 78 18 87.
19, rue de Turenne (4th). M° Saint-Paul.
Phone: 01 44 61 45 39.
delphinepariente.fr

VIVEKA BERGSTRÖM
LOVE OF VOLUME

Viveka's minimalist jewels are items that you will keep for a long time. She used to be a fashion designer, but now this Scandinavian creator, who has a love for volume, plays with golden or silver metal, Plexiglas, Swarovski crystals and mirrors. Everything is made in her studio and with local artisans.

23, rue de la Grange-aux-Belles (10th).
M° Colonel Fabien. Phone: 01 40 03 04 92.
viveka-bergstrom.blogspot.com

Viveka Bergström

FOR CHIC JEWELS IN SAINT-GERMAIN, LET'S MEET AT:

Adelline
For beautiful stones from India mounted on heavy, 22 carat gold.
54, rue Jacob (6th). M° Saint-Germain-des-Prés. Phone: 01 47 03 07 18. adelline.com
Stone
For tiny diamond and gold jewelry and cross earrings, all extremely refined.
60, rue des Saints-Pères (7th). M° Saint-Germain-des-Prés. Phone: 01 42 22 24 24. stoneparis.com
Ginette NY
For graphic creations, geometrical pendants and necklaces with messages.
66, rue des Saints-Pères (7th). M° Saint-Germain-des-Prés. Phone: 01 42 22 27 18. ginette-ny.com

CORPUS CHRISTI
ROCK DANDY

The body of Christ, the name fits perfectly the rock-dandy style of this Parisian brand! Their skull pendants, reliquaries, crowned hearts or gold, silver and silver-gilt guns can look more like Mexican ex-voto than steampunk accessories.

64, rue Vieille-du-Temple (3rd).

M° Hôtel de Ville, Saint-Paul. Phone: 01 42 77 15 55.

6, rue Ravignan (18th). M° Abbesses.

Phone: 01 42 57 77 77.

corpuschristi.fr

APRIATI
ON THREADS

Made in Athens, the jewels here are refined, made from silver, yellow, white or pink gold, mounted on colorful threads that circle the wrists, or paired with diamonds, precious stones or pearls. Originally located on the left bank and, more recently, on the right bank as well, the two boutiques magnificently display the pieces in big black windows.
So chic, and poetic.

310, rue Saint-Honoré (1st). M° Tuileries.

Phone: 01 42 60 10 10.

54, rue du Four (6th). M° Saint-Sulpice.

Phone: 01 42 22 15 42.

apriati.com

Corpus Christi

Apriati

RETRO
STATIONS
THE BEST OF VINTAGE CHIC AND FUN

BIS BOUTIQUE SOLIDAIRE
GENEROUS PIECES

Now displayed in two locations around Paris, this second hand clothes brand provides impeccable pieces from famous as well as unknown brands, at minimal prices. Here, the workers are in rehabilitation, and the clothes for women, men and children are collected by charities and given a second life.

7, boulevard du Temple (3rd). M° Filles du Calvaire.
Phone: 01 44 78 11 08.
19, rue Lamartine (9th).
M° Cadet, Notre-Dame-de-Lorette.
Phone: 09 67 60 97 94.
bisboutiquesolidaire.fr

Bis Boutique Solidaire

Odetta Vintage

ODETTA VINTAGE
FROM THE 1960'S TO THE 80'S

Here, beautiful designer pieces from the 1960's to the 80's, by Yves Saint Laurent, Azzaro or Lanvin, mix with a small selection of vintage furniture and lamps. The bonus: A few modern pieces of clothing harmonize perfectly with the rest. All of this is displayed in a positive atmosphere that makes you want to shop.

76, rue des Tournelles (3rd).
M° Chemin Vert.
Phone: 01 48 87 08 61.
odettavintage.com.

MAMIE BLUE ET MAMIE
THE ESSENTIAL

Retro fans of the capital are spreading the word on these two vintage shops. At number 69 on rue de Rochechouart, Mamie Blue displays pieces of 1920's to 70's fashion for men and women. Everything is impeccably restored. If you book, you can even get a complete hair and 50's makeup makeover. At Mamie's, number 73 on the same street, you will find second-hands: clothes from 1900 to 1980 are sold intact. Both boutiques also offer rentals – for your Gatsby-themed costume parties!

69, rue de Rochechouart (9th). M° Anvers.
Phone: 01 42 81 10 42.
73, rue de Rochechouart (9th). M° Anvers.
Phone: 01 42 82 09 98.
mamie-vintage.com

Mamie Blue

DO YOU WANT VINTAGE?

Here it is! The website Vintedge presents luxury vintage boutiques, knick-knack and second-hand shops in the City of Lights. It is constantly updated to keep up with the openings and closings.
What a precious ally for vintage fans!
thevintedge.com

Thanx God I'm a V.I.P.

THANX GOD I'M A V.I.P.
LUXURY VINTAGE
Spanning 2,000 square feet on the first floor and in a basement, luxury vintage pieces are designed by Céline, Gucci, Saint Laurent, etc. Rare and trendy clothes are arranged on the racks by color and print style.
This very specific selection is made by Sylvie Chateigner, the initiator of the famous parties "Thanx God I'm a V.I.P." On the website, you can see new arrivals and listen to a web radio.
12, rue de Lancry (10th).
M° République, Jacques Bonsergent.
Phone: 01 42 03 02 09.
thanxgod.com

PRETTY BOX
FOR THE HAPPY FEW
This is THE hub for vintage fashion, from the beginning of the century to the present! Sarah Cacoub Hazarosoff is a finder of rare and sublime pieces. And there are many of them here. The racks are cluttered, but you are sure to find what you are looking for. Plenty of fashion people, designers and models come here for inspiration.
46, rue de Saintonge (3rd).
M° Filles du Calvaire.
Phone: 01 48 04 81 71.
prettybox.fr

AND TO SELL?
From the outside, Violette & Léonie (114, rue de Turenne, 3rd. M° Filles du Calvaire. Phone: 01 44 59 87 35.) and La Cloackroom (14, rue des Taillandiers, 11th. M° Bastille, Ledru-Rollin. Phone: 01 77 18 25 42.) strangely resemble multibrand stores. But here, everything is second-hand, and half off.
On the left bank, Les Ginettes (4, rue du Sabot, 6th. M° Saint-Germain-des-Prés, Saint-Sulpice. Phone: 01 42 22 45 14.) mixes fashion and home design in a charming little dead-end street.
You can both buy and sell in these shops.

FASHION

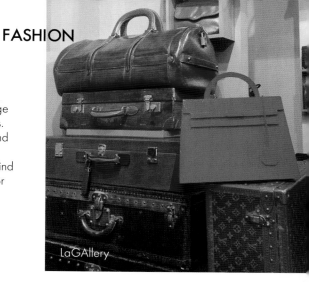

LaGAllery

LAGALLERY
RARE SKINS

This tiny place holds treasures of vintage leather goods from the 1920's to the 80's. The pieces are wonderfully preserved and are made from rare animal skins, such as ostrich, peccary and wild boar. You will find real crocodile clutches starting at 160€ or a leather Kelly at less than 3000€.
If you ask him, Guillaume can also do a search for your dream bag.
50, rue de Lille (7th). M° Rue du Bac, Solférino. Phone: 01 72 34 81 50. lagallery.fr

LA JOLIE GARDE-ROBE
CRAZY STOCKS

Marie Rouches is a compulsive bargain hunter and a fan of beautiful labels. In twenty years, she has compiled a crazy stock of items that she is slowly selling off in her little store of north Marais. You will find rare pieces from the 1920's to the 90's, some of which have never been worn. With or without a label, they seduce designers and fashionistas alike. A gold mine for fashion enthusiasts!
15, rue Commines (3rd). M° Filles du Calvaire. Phone: 01 42 72 13 90.

COME BACK
SECOND-HAND PASSION

A movie costume designer with an everlasting passion for second-hand clothing runs the Come Back. She loved vintage even before we called it that! Printed velvet jackets, hand-knitted Irish sweaters, Liberty corsages from the 1970's – she selects one item at a time, never in bundles. This results in consistency of style and provides well-preserved clothing.
51, rue des Orteaux (20th). M° Maraîchers, Alexandre Dumas. Phone: 06 85 07 46 96.

Come Back

WHAT A CONCEPT STORE!

PLACES THAT ARE NOTHING LIKE THE REST

Marché Noir

MARCHĒ NOIR
AMUSEMENT AND REFINEMENT

The team from the Comptoir Général opened this surprising space, which splits its 7,500 square feet between a selective second-hand shop and a restaurant / tea-house. On the store side, trunks full of clothes convey an African vibe. On the bar side, a 1920's colonial atmosphere reigns. The interior design expresses amusement and refinement through every detail – for instance, in the "ostrich eggs" suspensions or in the ceiling lights made from doormats. The change of scene is guaranteed, and you can have fresh fruit cocktails.
18, rue Perrée (3rd). M° Temple.

LEKKER KKONCEPT STORE
MULTITASK

Fashion, art, home and cafeteria! This boutique may be small, but nonetheless it is rich. A creation wall is dedicated to a different artist every three months, the furniture is vintage, and you can find jewels, clutches and home decor accessories. In the hallway that leads to the kitchen, fashion items from a few Parisian designers are displayed on a rack. On the table (which is for sale), you can enjoy the proprietor's homemade daily special.
35, rue des Trois-Frères (18th). M° Abbesses.
lekker.fr

Lekker Kkoncept Store

KLIN D'ŒIL
SHOPPING AND WORKSHOP

Ephemeral boutiques were organized by the sisters Emilie and Virginie Capman before they decided to settle and showcase their favorite designers in this pretty store.
On one side, you will find their selection of jewels, bags, scarfs, cushions and ceramics. On the other side, a huge table where you can talk to the designers while drinking coffee, and participate in the workshops that take place on Saturdays: silkscreen printing, natural dye, silk painting, etc.
6, rue Deguerry (11th). M° Goncourt.
Phone: 01 77 15 22 30.
klindoeil.com

SERGE BENSIMON
FASHION AND HOME DESIGNER

HIS CONCEPT STORE
INES DE LA FRESSANGE PARIS
"Our famous Ines gathered in one place a selection that looks like her. I love it, bravo!"
24, rue de Grenelle (7TH).
M° Saint-Sulpice, Rue du Bac.
Phone: 01 45 48 19 06.
inesdelafressange.fr

MEL, MICH & MARTIN
WINNING TRIO

Fashion, food and home design mix wonderfully in this hybrid place. On the fashion and home decor side, items by unknown French designers are featured in a vintage setting that is for sale too.
On the food side, fresh products straight from Normandy are turned into delicious bagels, tarts, healthy salads, cheesecakes, banana-caramel cake, etc. Everything is a delight! Not to mention the huge terrace.
8, rue Saint-Bernard (11th). M° Faidherbe-Chaligny.
Phone: 01 73 71 79 04. melmichetmartin.paris

NOYOCO
HIPSTER'S PARADISE

This young ready-made brand presents mixed clothing in its concept store: draped wool pants, coats that can be worn different ways, hats and sweatshirts with hipster messages. The cuts are perfect and the details are chic. We love their selection of home decor items that includes international magazines, books and candles. A great spot!

41, rue des Dames (17th).
M° Rome, Place de Clichy.
Phone: 01 74 30 58 30.
noyoco.com

LE SOUK PARISIEN
SMALL PRICES

This concept store offers minimal prices and a varied selection: fine foods to honor regional French specialties, games for children, plenty of designer jewelry, fashion and home decor accessories, notebooks, high-tech gadgets, etc. Truly original.

199, rue du Faubourg-Saint-Antoine (11th).
M° Faidherbe Chaligny.
Phone: 01 43 57 07 84.
lesoukparisien.fr

INES DE LA FRESSANGE
FASHION AND
HOME DESIGNER

HER CONCEPT STORE
MONA MARKET
"It is ideal for home decor. The selection of objects and home furniture is simply perfect. I love the ethnic-chic vibe conveyed by Made by Tinja's pottery."

4, rue de Commines (3rd).
M° Saint-Sébastien Froissart,
Filles du Calvaire.
Phone: 01 42 78 80 04.
monamarket.com

FRONT DE MODE
EXPERIMENTAL STORE
Created by fashion designer Sakina M'sa,
this experimental store gathers about fifty designers involved in fair trade (with a social approach to production, and eco-friendly products). The 2,000-square-foot space also includes a place to read and have a light lunch, a mini-gallery and a studio where you can order tailor-made jeans in the denim of your choice.

42, rue Volta (3rd). M° Arts et Métiers, Temple.
Phone: 09 80 63 16 33.
frontdemode.com

FRENCH TOUCHE
A PROFUSION OF PRETTY
An iconic place in Batignolles,
this "gallery of meaningful objects" gathers the pretty ready-made items by Charlotte Sometime, local fashion designer pieces, and Unseven silkscreen printed T-shirts to honor dead rock stars. Is this all? No, there are also retro toys for children, numerous notebooks, beautiful jewelry, ceramics, books and records!

90, rue Legendre (17th).
M° Brochant, La Fourche.
Phone: 01 42 63 31 36.
frenchtouche.com

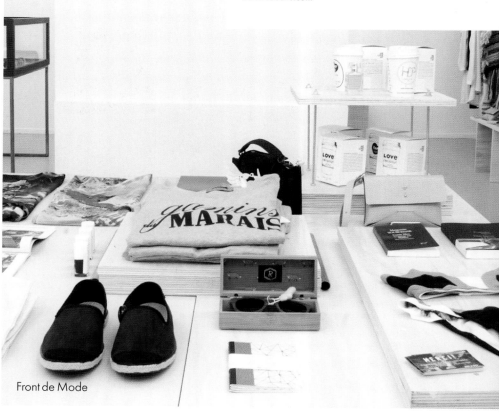

Front de Mode

Mint & Lilies

MINT & LILIES
PLANTS, FASHION AND HOME DECOR

Mint & Lilies was founded by two bloggers.
It is full of small decor objects, tableware, lamps, cushions, mirrors and furniture (bargain-hunted or ethnic, ranging from school chairs to Moroccan benches). It also has a beautiful fashion corner with clothes, bags and jewelry, as well as a selection of plants, dried flowers, garlands and cacti. This place is a poetic bubble in the Denfert-Rochereau neighborhood.
27-29, rue Daguerre (14th).
M° Denfert-Rochereau, Mouton Duvernet.
Phone: 01 43 35 30 25.

BRAZILINI
TROPICAL TRAVEL

This 100 percent Brazil-oriented store is full of Brazilian know-hows, known brands and young talents. You will discover the amazing cosmetics by Granado, Juliana Curi's graphic cushions and the Chocolate Q chocolate. This tropical trip brightens up every day Paris.
38, rue Greneta (2nd). M° Étienne Marcel, Sentier.
Phone: 09 83 24 25 35.
brazilini.com

BABEL CONCEPT STORE
A CHIC MIX

On the bank of the canal Saint-Martin,
the large windows of this concept store feature men and women's fashion, numerous accessories and jewelry. The selection goes well with the new and vintage home decor objects, the stationery, homemade terrariums and organic cosmetics. Here, the focus is on French designs.
55, quai de Valmy (10th).
M° République, Jacques Bonsergent.
Phone: 01 42 40 10 95.
babelconceptstore.com

Gab & Jo

FASHION

Babel Concept Store

GAB & JO
THE FRENCH WAY
This store is more than just a place that sells items made in France – it is the hub for French know-how and good taste. More than two hundred fashion and home decor brands are represented here, as well as everyday objects for adults and kids, including toys and books.
28, rue Jacob (6th). M° Saint-Germain-des-Prés.
Phone: 09 84 53 58 43.
gabjo.fr

MADE BY MOI
FROM ALL OVER
This place should not be mistaken for a do-it-yourself workshop. Made by moi's two boutiques gather designers from all fields: fashion (Idano, CKS), jewelry (Anne Thomas, Tambour Paris), bags (Julie Meuriss, Antoinette Ameska), home decor (House Doctor, La Bougie Française, Germaines) and high tech with Kreafunk stereos and headsets.
71, rue du Faubourg-Saint-Martin (10th).
M° Château d'Eau, Jacques Bonsergent.
Phone: 09 83 01 30 07.
86, rue Oberkampf, (11th).
M° Parmentier.
Phone: 01 58 30 95 78.
madebymoi.fr.

LES JAVOTTES
MADE IN LE SENTIER
Lorraine Mordillat offers an affordable selection in fashion (ready-made, shoes, bags and jewels), and home design (tableware, stationery, metal bins). Her secret? She picks brands that are made locally in Le Sentier, such as La Petite Française ready-made garments, as well as lesser-known French and foreign designers. The Eponyme boots in particular are so pretty!
48, rue Greneta (2nd). M° Étienne Marcel, Sentier.
Phone: 01 40 26 53 71.

LA BOTIKE BELGE
STORIES FROM BELGIUM
An old corsetry called Claverie was changed into this joyful Belgium grocer-shop. Sweet and savory products, beers, bargain-hunted furniture, coffee-table books, fashion designs, and silverware can be found here.
234, rue du Faubourg-Saint-Martin (10th). M° Louis Blanc.
Phone: 09 81 15 12 82. gabjo.fr

PIMP YOUR
GUY

WHERE TO GO TO GIVE YOUR MAN A MAKEOVER

Balibaris

WAIT
FOR SURFERS

This store was opened by Antoine Mocquard and Julien Tual, the designers of Waiting For The Sun glasses, Bois 2, Slash and a ready-made brand made in France. It is the go-to place for surfing enthusiasts, featuring high-tech boards, outdoor technical clothing, records, books, specialized magazines – all of this in a feels-like-home place with a couch and a living room.

9, rue Notre-Dame-de-Nazareth (3rd).

M° Temple, République. Phone: 09 82 52 84 34.

waitingforthesun.fr

BALIBARIS
REVISITING CLASSICS

It all began with ties, which revolutionized the chic look. Then, little by little, a whole wardrobe full of classics has been revisited here to dress men from head to toe. The prices are reasonable, and the store communicates freely on the European manufacturing process. This young brand now owns ten stores in Paris – a sure sign of their success!

Addresses on balibaris.com

LÉON FLAM
A HERITAGE

In this workshoplike boutique, the young designer revives leather travel bags originally created by his grandfather. You will also find accessories in limited editions, shoes, some ready-made items and a customization service.

6, rue des Filles du Calvaire (3rd).

M° Filles du Calvaire.

Phone: 01 42 76 92 98.

leonflam.com

Wait

V.B.S. BARBER & SHOP
THE BEARD
This boutique features casual-chic fashion from all over the world, as well as a barbershop window with excellent products.
96, rue du Faubourg-Poissonnière (10ᵉ). M° Poissonnière.
Phone: 01 40 16 40 20. vbarberandshop.com

PHM Saints Pères

LA GARÇONNIÈRE
ALL FOR HIM
The founders of APTO, Monsieur London, Newstalk and Oncle Pape launched this 2,700-square-foot concept store in the middle of Le Sentier. It features fashion items, accessories, beauty products, fine foods, lifestyle objects, a barbershop and even a coffee shop. It is also open on Sundays from 1:30 p.m. to 6 p.m.
40, rue des Petits-Carreaux (2ⁿᵈ). M° Sentier.
Phone: 09 73 68 14 47.
la-garconniere.fr

PHM SAINTS PÈRES
BIG NAMES
This nicely designed multibrand store highlights top-of-the-line brands in contemporary fashion, exclusive productions by big names of the milieu, and original shirts created by the founder of the place, Pierre-Henri Mattout.
50, rue des Saints-Pères (6ᵗʰ). M° Saint-Germain-des-Prés.
Phone: 09 67 18 47 28.
phmsaintsperes.com

La Garçonnière

La GARÇONNIÈRE

SAUVER LE MONDE DES HOMMES
COOL DANDIES

Close to the canal Saint-Martin, in the Marais, in Montmartre and soon in la Villette, this multibrand seduces Parisian dandies with five principles: to establish oneself (with fashion), to arm oneself (with accessories), to take care of oneself (with beauty products), savor (with fine foods) and to preserve oneself (with toys, books and objects). Watch this space!

42, rue Saint-Antoine (4th). M° Bastille, Saint-Paul.
Phone: 09 82 22 97 53.
8, rue Beaurepaire (10th). M° République.
Phone: 09 84 51 86 12.
sauverlemondedeshommes.com

SHOP FROM HOME

With Georges, you can obtain help from a private stylist who is connected to the biggest menswear e-shop: menlook.com. You create a profile and answer a few questions before being contacted by a stylist. The latter will shop the 350 brands available on menlook.com and send you a selection. You will have ten days to make a decision and send back what you don't like with the delivery-person who turns up at your door. The prices are communicated on menlook.com, and you pay for only what you keep.

georgesprive.com

ÉCLECTIC
HIGH-TECH CLASS

This shop is surprising in that it sells jackets and coats that mix technology and tradition. The fabric is borrowed from the world of sports, and it is altogether innovative, efficient, ultra light, breathing and resistant. The designs are handmade by a master tailor from Treviso. They are elegant and functional, and prices start at 650€.

8, rue Charlot (3rd). M° Filles du Calvaire.
Phone: 01 42 78 00 20.
e-eclectic.com

éclectic

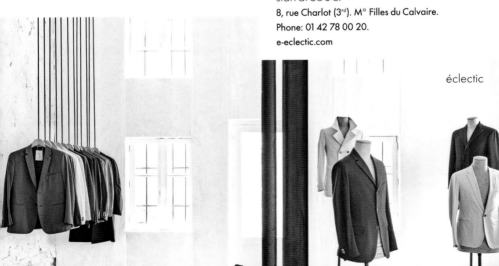

FASHION

Commune de Paris, 1871

COMMUNE DE PARIS, 1871
A COMPLETE DRESSING ROOM

A chic to casual range of clothes is offered by the designer duo Alexandre Maïsetti and Sébastien Lucky for each season, large enough to fill an entire dressing room. It includes artists' silk-screen printed shirts as well as products from very successful new partnerships – for example, with Astier de Villatte or Lip watches.

19, rue Commines (3rd). M° Filles du Calvaire. Phone: 09 81 90 13 37. Communedeparis1871.fr

ATELIERS AUGUSTE
URBAN GOODS

Bags adapted to city life and that are also chic accessories are the goals that challenged the two founding brothers when designing their products, all made in the French region of Vendée. Their waxed waterproof cotton and full grain leather designs borrow their names from different quarters of Paris: Montorgueil bag, Verneuil briefcase, Valmy saddlebag, etc.

8, rue de Turenne (4th). M° Saint-Paul.

Phone: 01 48 05 91 36.

ateliers-auguste.fr

A TAILOR-MADE STYLIST

With Chictypes, you register online and book a phone meeting with a stylist who will enquire about the tastes, needs, sizes and budget of the man you want to dress.
A few days later, a trunk full of clothes and accessories by Paul Smith, Levi's, Scotch & Soda, The Kooples, etc. is delivered to your door.
You can keep the trunk for seven days, try everything on, send back what you don't like and pay (store prices) for only the items you keep!
chictypes.com

SIX & SEPT
TO SEE VENICE

This young Parisian brand is devoted to knitwear exclusively: superfine merino wool in winter, and Egyptian cotton in summer. The designs are thought up in the 16th, and knitted in a Venetian studio. Items range from essentials to fun creations.

11, rue de Sévigné (4th). M° Saint-Paul.

Phone: 01 43 48 89 37.

27 bis, rue Duret (16th). M° Argentine.

Phone: 09 54 41 38 25.

sixetsept.fr

CUISSE DE GRENOUILLE
MIX AND REMIX

Ties, T-shirts, socks, swimwear

are combined with coffee-table books and well-chosen gadgets in these three Parisian boutiques. The last one was first devoted to beachwear, but has since converted to selling women's clothing.

5, rue Froissart (3rd). Phone: 09 51 27 85 86.

104, rue Vieille-du-Temple (3rd).

Phone: 09 72 86 65 30.

M° Saint-Sébastien Froissart.

71, place du Docteur-Félix-Lobligeois (17th).

M° Brochant, Rome.

Phone: 09 52 75 41 93.

cuissedegrenouille.com

Six & Sept

FASHION

Ami

PIGALLE
YOUNG PRODIGY

Every fashion guru will tell you this:
Keep an eye open for Stéphane Ashpool and
his two clothing lines. The first one is in wool,
mohair or leather. The second one is street-
inspired: nylon jackets, graphic sweatshirts and
T-shirts. Both have nice colors and are
beautifully manufactured.
7, rue Henri-Monnier (9th). M° Saint-Georges.
Phone: 01 48 78 59 74.
pigalle-paris.com

LE SLIP FRANÇAIS
A CRAZY SENSE OF HUMOR

Briefs, boxers, underpants but also swimsuits,
socks, slippers, espadrilles, T-shirts, etc.
The items from this French-made brand have a
crazy sense of humor and an offbeat style.
137, rue Vieille-du-Temple (3rd). M° Filles du Calvaire,
Saint-Sébastien Froissart. Phone: 01 42 77 92 79.
20, rue du Vieux-Colombier (6th). M° Saint-Sulpice.
46, rue des Abbesses (18th). M° Abbesses.
Phone: 01 42 59 99 42.
leslipfrancais.fr

AMI
ALEXANDER THE GREAT

**Alexandre Mattiussi is basking in his
success** with a laid-back urban chic style and
the opening of three stores in Paris.
14, rue d'Alger (1st). M° Tuileries.
Phone: 09 82 44 40 20.
109, boulevard Beaumarchais (3rd).
M° Saint-Sébastien Froissart.
Phone: 09 83 27 65 28.
22, rue de Grenelle (7th).
M° Saint-Sulpice, Sèvres-Babylone.
Phone: 09 82 30 96 77.
amiparis.fr

Le Slip Français

BEAUTY AND HEALTH

THE PARISIAN WOMAN IS VERY BUSY, BUT SHE ALWAYS FINDS THE TIME TO TAKE **CARE** OF HERSELF!

ECO-**PRETTY**

PLACES FOR YOUR SKIN,
YOUR HAIR AND THE PLANET

Weleda

WELEDA
AN OASIS

Particularly appreciated for its cosmetics
(made from musk rose, iris or almond) and its
medicinal products (arnica oil, sea-buckthorn
syrup), this boutique was conceived with an eco-
friendly mind and is an oasis dedicated to their
customers' well-being. Massages, face and
body treatments as well as courses to learn how
to massage your baby and yourself are all available here. 45 min face massage for 70€.
10, avenue Franklin-D.-Roosevelt (8th).
M° Saint-Philippe-du-Roule, Frankin D. Roosevelt.
Phone: 01 53 96 06 15.
weleda.fr

DR. HAUSCHKA
PROTOCOOL

In its Feng Shui institute La Maison
or in its store La Closeraie, the German
brand appeals with its products and natural
beauty treatments. Hats off to initiatives
such as the facial gym, which firms up your
face and prevents wrinkles without
having to use cosmetics! 129€ for
three sessions.
Store: 9, rue Pierre-Dupont (10th).
M° Louis Blanc, Château-Landon.
Phone: 01 43 55 45 50.
Institute: 39, rue de Charonne (11th).
M° Ledru-Rollin, Bastille.
Phone: 01 43 55 40 55.
dr.hauschka.com

Dr. Hauschka

Les Belles Plantes

LES BELLES PLANTES
REBIRTH

In her salon, Gaëlle takes good care of your hair, completely restoring its natural splendor after years of bad treatments (aggressive dyes and shampoos). Once you have chosen a color, she adds a vegetable dye while giving you precious advice on at-home treatments and recipes. Coloring prices range from 70 to 115€, and the cut is 55€.

15, rue Jean-Macé (11th). M° Charonne.
Phone: 01 43 72 87 70. lesbellesplantes.fr

AROMA-ZONE
DO IT YOURSELF

On the first floor of the huge boutique Aroma-Zone, all of the ingredients required to prepare your own organic and natural beauty products are available: plant extracts, essential oil, cosmetic actives and even bottles. Upstairs, there is a studio where you can learn how to make the recipes, and a spa to experiment tailor-made treatments.

25, rue de l'École-de-Médecine (6th).
M° Odéon.
Phone: 01 43 26 08 93.
aroma-zone.com

Korres

BIOCOIFF' BY CHARLEY
VEGETABLE HAIR DYE

Charley and his team only believe in vegetable hair dyes. The real organic ones that fix hair worn down by years of chemical use. If you cannot go there, you can get an online diagnosis and order an at-home coloring kit. At the shop, dyeing treatments pricing starts at 108€ (93€ for a regular dye).

5, rue des Ciseaux (6th). M° Saint-Germain-des-Prés, Mabillon. Phone: 01 43 26 77 77.
19, place Jeanne-d'Arc (13th). M° Olympiades.
Phone: 01 45 85 91 09. biocoiff.com

KORRES
MADE IN GREECE

Inspired by treatments in Athens, pharmacist and homeopath George Korres has created enchanting packaging and uses ingredients such as olive oil, thyme and rosemary. The plants' active ingredients are soft and safe for your skin, and the products are free of any synthetic components such as paraben and any animal products.

54, rue des Écoles (5th).
M° Maubert-Mutualité, Cluny-La Sorbonne.
Phone: 01 43 26 83 34.
korres.fr

SECRET
MASSAGES
EXOTIC PLACES TO RELAX

Yuzuka

YUZUKA
READY FOR YUZU?

This beautiful place is dedicated to Japanese well-being and offers virtuous products made from yuzu. You are left in firm and delicate hands, and can let yourself go during your lymphatic massage, shiatsu, foot reflexology, abdominal detox or firming face treatment. Prices start at 45€ for 30min. Their wonderful idea was to offer lunch specials of bento + massage or after work specials for women in a hurry.

62, avenue Bosquet (7th).
M° École Militaire.
Phone: 09 83 93 83 41.
yuzuka.fr

Ban Thaï Spa

BAN THAÏ SPA
AN ATMOSPHERE OF CHOICE

Nothing is better to get you back up on your feet than a Thai massage. At Ban Thaï Spa, you have the privilege to choose between a contemporary or authentic atmosphere, depending on the location. Our favorite is the Montorgueil spa, where the ambience of Bangkok spas is perfectly re-created. Whatever your choice, you will be impressed, particularly by the foot reflexology treatment, which starts at 75€ an hour.

Addresses on paris-massage.fr

LA MAISON DU TUI NA
DEEP

This traditional Chinese massage allows for a better flow of energy and blood. The masseur kneads the body, loosens knots and stimulates energy points from head to toe. This deep massage is affordable (60€ for an hour) and exists in a range of different types: thinning, firming, detox, etc.

13, rue Saint-Gilles (3rd). M° Chemin Vert.
Phone: 01 42 77 70 38.
14, rue Duvivier (7th). M° La Tour-Maubourg, École Militaire.
Phone: 01 45 55 02 61.
9, rue Nicolo (16th). M° Passy.
Phone: 01 45 24 53 89.
lamaisondutuina.fr

MONT KAILASH
STIMULATING

Massages, face treatments, eyebrow thinning, manicures, pedicures, meditation and yoga classes – Tibetan beauty has two institutes in Paris. We recommend the stimulating massage Traditional Tibetan Art (117€ for 70 min) that frees all energies.

16, rue Saint-Marc (2nd).
M° Richelieu-Drouot, Bourse.
Phone: 01 42 36 03 30.
19, rue Pierre-Leroux (7th). M° Vaneau.
Phone: 01 53 86 94 73.
montkailash-bien-etre.fr

Lanqi Spa

LANQI SPA
ANCESTRAL

With great service and minimal prices, Lanqi Spa is the spot that ELLE journalists share with each other. Lanqi and her team have inherited ancestral knowledge and know-hows, and practice massages from traditional Chinese medicine. Try out the "Tui Na," which works well for backaches. From 48€ for a one-hour massage.

48, avenue de Saxe (7th). M° Ségur.
Phone: 01 44 38 72 05 and 01 47 83 52 72.
91, rue de Javel (15th).
M° Charles Michels.
Phone: 01 45 79 63 67.
lanqi-spa.com

A TREATMENT AT HOME

Beauty at home has become very accessible through apps and websites, such as monbeaumiroir.paris, popmyday.fr and mymec.fr. Make-up, hair, waxing, body and face treatments, manicures, the services offered are plenty, at reasonable prices, and with the possibility of paying online. They are available seven days a week – no more excuses!

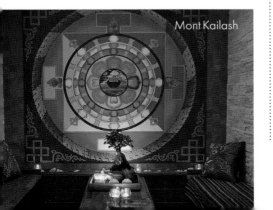

Mont Kailash

FULL STEAM **AHEAD**

THE BEST STEAM ROOMS TO HANG OUT WITH THE GIRLS

O'Kari

CHARME D'ORIENT
LIKE IN A FAIRYTALE

Yasmina, of Algerian descent, unveils the secrets of Middle Eastern beauty through her line of cosmetics. To honor her products made from natural and traditional ingredients, she opened close to République the prettiest steam room in all Paris. It is a gem that makes you feel like you are in a fairytale from *The Arabian Nights!* The exfoliating treatment starts at 49€ for 30 min.

18, boulevard du Temple (11th).
M° Filles du Calvaire, République.
Phone: 01 53 17 02 53.
charmedorient.fr

O'KARI
POCKET HAMMAM

At the end of a courtyard in the middle of Montorgueil, who would dream of finding a pocket steam room? This is also an address we exchange at work at ELLE. We go there for a honey-rose petal or clay envelopment, an oil shampoo that leaves us with dream hair, and we prolong our relaxation time with a Middle Eastern cake and mint tea. Envelopments from 60€.

22, rue Dussoubs (2nd).
M° Réaumur-Sébastopol, Étienne Marcel.
Phone: 01 42 36 94 66.
o-kari.com

LES CENT CIELS
MIXED OR NOT

This steam room is more intimate than its cousin in Boulogne, and takes you to the land of *The Arabian Nights.* Dimmed lights, Middle Eastern paintings, honey-colored tiles — all the ingredients are here. Between a black soap exfoliating treatment and a dip in the pool, you can even go for a bath in donkey milk. The bonus? Some days and at certain times, the place is mixed (swimsuit required).

7, rue de Nemours (11th). M° Parmentier, Oberkampf.
Phone: 01 55 28 95 75.
hammam-lescentciels.com

Charme d'Orient

BEAUTY AND HEALTH

HAMMAM PACHA
RELAX WITH YOUR FRIENDS
With its all white setting, this place is the ideal spot to meet up for a relaxing time with your girlfriends. There is plenty of space in the steam room. A firming black soap exfoliating treatment, a mint green tea, an organic meal, Pacha offers a mini-trip to Marrakech! Basic package with exfoliating treatment: 60€.

17, rue Mayet (6th). M° Duroc, Falguière.
Phone: 01 43 06 55 55. hammampacha.com

LES SOURCES DE L'ORIENT
NATURAL TREATMENTS
This small welcoming steam room was rebuilt three years ago. Azulejos on the walls, treatments with natural Middle Eastern products, kind personnel, whether you pick a traditional rhassoul or argan oil wrapping or an oxygen face treatment, you will come out regenerated, body and soul.
Relaxing massages start at 49€.

17, rue des Acacias (17th).
M°Argentine.
Phone: 01 44 09 85 79.
les-sources-del-orient.com

LA SULTANE DE SABA
JOURNEY OF THE SENSES
Whichever address you choose, the 2nd arrondissement location or the 16th, both take you on a journey of the senses. In a setting with bronze mosaics on the walls and crystal chandeliers, you can try out the classic treatment: exfoliating with rose salt, rhassoul and shea butter wraping and an oil massage. Where to? Depending on the perfume you choose, you can travel to India, Maghreb, Japan. Body treatments start at 49€.

8 bis, rue Bachaumont (2nd). M° Sentier, Étienne Marcel.
Phone: 01 40 41 90 95.
78, rue Boissière (16th). M° Victor Hugo.
Phone: 01 45 00 00 40.
lasultanedesaba.com

La Sultane de Saba

TREATMENTS FOR
SMOOTH SKIN

THE BEST BEAUTY SALONS
FOR A RADIANT FACE

NEOMIST
PROFESSIONAL DIAGNOSES

Neomist specializes in face treatments
in this unique Parisian place. It is particularly
appreciated for its lotion with natural active
ingredients that penetrates the skin instantly.
Get a skin diagnosis there and treat yourself to
skincare, or get a personalized formula.
A 20-minute treatment costs 40€.

29, rue Notre-Dame-de-Nazareth (3rd).
M° Temple, République.
Phone: 01 42 78 44 47.
neomist-linstitut-paris.fr

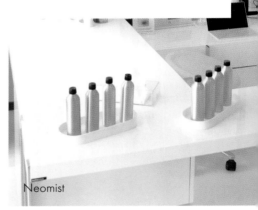

Neomist

Marinel Institut

MARINEL INSTITUT
FACELIFT EFFECT

Older women know this place for its
oxygen and vitamin treatments that
deeply hydrate and nourish the skin.
Their treatments provide a facelift
effect without having surgery. They
also sell the Clinicare line of products
to continue this rejuvenating effect at
home. The oxygen treatment costs
250€ for 1h30.

267, rue Saint-Honoré (1st).
M° Concorde, Madeleine.
Phone: 09 54 90 78 31.
marinel.fr

BEAUTY AND HEALTH

Maison Codage Paris

MAISON CODAGE PARIS
AT THE FOREFRONT

This young brand received plenty of attention for its new generation line of serums. Their formulas are at the forefront of technology; they brighten your skin tone, smooth the lines on your face and prepare your skin for seasonal changes. After receiving a diagnosis, you can opt for a tailor-made serum or leave with a ready-to-use product, a little less specific but certainly cheaper. Tailor-made treatments start at 75€ for an hour.

8, rue du Trésor (4th).
M° Saint-Paul, Hôtel de Ville. Phone: 01 40 27 80 09.
codageparis.com

INSTITUT PALOMA
MAGNIFYING GLASS

This is a charming beauty salon, far from the restlessness of the Champs-Elysées. Inside the sober but comfortable cubicles, you can get waxed, get your makeup done, have a mani-pedi and go for tailor-made face treatments. After a deep analysis of your skin with Derma Vizualiser (70€), the beautician applies the appropriate Babor treatments to your skin. This starts at 75€. It is instructive and beneficial.

17, rue de la Trémoille (8th). M° Alma-Marceau, Franklin D. Roosevelt. Phone: 01 47 20 10 63.
institutpaloma.com

Institut Paloma

Seymour Projects

A HEALTHY MIND

At Seymour Projects, you are invited to leave your phone, computer, books and other visual distractions behind, and embark on a mental journey. Five spaces are designed to help your mind wander and rediscover the benefits of reflection and introspection. Fun and rewarding! Suggested donation: 7€.

41, boulevard de Magenta (10th).
M° Jacques Bonsergent, Gare de l'Est.
Phone: 01 40 03 81 68. seymourprojects.com

e-clat

LES PETITS SOINS
SUCCESS STORY

Claire Martichoux's beauty salons offer a warm welcome, specific treatments and pretty designs, a successful combination. Six locations exist already, and everyone rushes there for the Françoise Morice Kinéplastie, a mind-blowing hand-delivered smoothing treatment (98€), the Kure Bazaar manicure (30€), the palpate-roll zone massage (58€ for one 45-minute session, or 300€ for 6 sessions), or waxing treatments (21€ for a half leg).

Six addresses on petitssoins.fr

E-CLAT
FROM THE ENTIRE WORLD

In a perfectly white setting, this place gathers famous cosmetics from the entire world. It also includes a men's corner, a beauty bar for makeup advice or a manicure (starts at 25€), a skin bar where you can get a skin diagnosis and a cubicle to receive three exclusive Esthederm tailor-made treatments, for cleansing, against skin dysfunctions, for brightness and youth (from 37 to 83€). Once a month, a special evening is planned with clients where beauty tips are given. An impressive beauty store!

90, rue de Richelieu (2nd).
M° Bourse, Richelieu-Drouot.
Phone: 01 49 27 99 91.
e-clat.fr

BEAUTY AND HEALTH

ERBORIAN
FRENCH-KOREAN

Korean women are experts at cosmetics, and we are only just starting to discover their secrets, thanks to this French-Korean brand. Forty-five references are presented and classified into three major steps: cleaning, treating (serums, masks, cream) and makeup. They notably sell the famous CC HD Cream. At the BB Bar, you can learn how to apply the products correctly.

45, avenue de l'Opéra (2nd).
M° Opéra, Quatre-Septembre.
Phone: 01 42 33 35 64.
fr.erborian.com

Jane de Busset

Erborian

JANE DE BUSSET
PURIFYING

Sylvie Puig's beauty salon is hidden in an apartment; it is the place to share with your girlfriends. Go there for the "Hydradermie" treatment, a deep cleansing with chemical removal of deposits associated to a galvanic current and high frequency disinfectant, which also includes a massage, mask, shower (around 138€). You can also go there for light peels or invigorating treatments, and come out as good as new! To extend the effect, Sylvie developed a line of products made to order.

30, rue Pasquier (8th).
M° Saint-Augustin, Havre-Caumartin.
Phone: 01 42 65 53 55.
janedebusset.com

WELL-NEGOTIATED TREATMENTS

Ask for a service online (manicure, haircut, wax, massage) and receive a negotiated offer from three Parisian salons within 24 hours. All you have left to do is book an appointment. On the app, you can access treatments immediately available near you at negotiated prices.
App free on App Store and Google Play.
pour-moi.fr

HANDS
AND FEET!

CHARMING SPOTS FOR
WONDERFUL MANI-PEDIS

JOĒ INSTITUT
CHIC AND COZY

Close to the Monceau park, Christelle and her team welcome you in their chic and cozy salon. There is a space with two round tables, a large couch full of cushions and Moroccan-inspired tanks for mani-pedis (hands + feet + polish for 60€). The are three cubicles right next to this space for waxing and face treatments (signature treatment: 80€ for an hour).
5, rue Médéric (17th). M° Courcelles.
Phone: 01 46 22 03 20.
joe-institut.fr

Joé Institut

NAIL CLUB
NAIL ART

Nadine designed her Nail Club as a welcoming loft, with brick walls, a long table and ceiling lights. You can go there to learn nail art, to get a manicure or pedicure. The atmosphere is always friendly. Her bright idea was to offer a room that you can rent to organize your own private "Nail Art Parties" with your girlfriends. Polish care: 10€.
134, rue Saint-Maur (11th).
M° Couronnes, Goncourt.
Phone: 09 82 51 33 75.
nailclub.fr

VERNISSAGE
OPEN UNTIL 9 P.M.

This place has been chosen by the ELLE editorial board as one of the best nail places in Paris. It is open until 9 p.m. from Monday to Friday – very convenient for working girls!
As a bonus, the owner's sister can blow-dry your hair right around the corner.
Get an express makeover by experts.
Manicure at 32€.
33, avenue de la Motte-Picquet (7th).
M° École Militaire.
Phone: 01 45 51 67 71.
vernissage-paris.com

BEAUTY AND HEALTH

AT HOME!

Rebecca travels all around Paris with a luggage full of Kure Bazaar and O.P.I. products. Gentle and professional, she adds thin layer upon thin layer of polish for a chic result and an impeccable hold for over a week. A service that is not more expensive than in a salon. It starts at 60€ for a manicure + pedicure.

Book at 06 24 10 21 00 or by email at rebecca.manucure@gmail.com

FREE PERSEPHONE
COTTAGE ATMOSPHERE

This salon looks like a cottage in spring, with guest tables under a tree for manicures (starts at 34€), floral chairs where you can curl up during your pedicure (starts at 51€), a cubicle with a view on the courtyard for face and body treatments (starts at 68€) and delightful perfumes made in Grasse. The kitchen serves as a gourmet teahouse.

66, boulevard Raspail (6th).

M° Rennes.

Phone: 01 42 22 13 04.

freepersephone.com

Free Persephone

Kure Bazaar

KURE BAZAAR
IN COLOR

Located under the roof of the Park Hyatt, the organic polish brand Kure Bazaar welcomes you in suite 601. Its natural products made from wood, cotton and corn pulp stay on just as long as non-organic products. This secret place has a refined design, just like the sixty nuances in the color chart. During your manicure, you will feel like a V.I.P.! Hand treatments start at 50€.

5, rue de la Paix (2nd).

M° Opéra.

Phone: 01 58 71 12 34.

ALTERNATIVE
COSMETICS
THE MOST ORIGINAL BOUTIQUES

Graine de pastel

OFFICINE UNIVERSELLE
BULY 1803
OLD-FASHIONED

This magnificent boutique is inspired by eighteenth-century perfumeries. Here, you will find wonderful items and beauty accessories by Buly — an iconic house since 1803 — along with a potpourri bar that includes thousands of secrets from all over the world: baobab seed oil for dry skin, iris root powder to brighten your skin tone, etc.

6, rue Bonaparte (6th).
M° Saint-Germain-des-Prés.
Phone: 01 43 29 02 50.
buly1803.com

GRAINE DE PASTEL
NEW TREATMENTS

Nathalie Juin and Carole Garcia, the creators of this brand, have given the south-western plant called "woad" a new purpose. The plant is commonly used to produce a blue dye. Its seeds are full of active nutritive chemicals and had never been used in cosmetics before. You can now discover this product in their line of treatments, available in two Parisian boutiques. At the 6th arrondissement store, you can even try out the products in a cubicle.

18, rue Pavée (4th). M° Saint-Paul. Phone: 01 84 06 62 45.
18, rue du Dragon (6th). M° Saint-Germain-des-Prés, Saint-Sulpice. Phone: 01 43 25 61 53.
grainedepastel.com

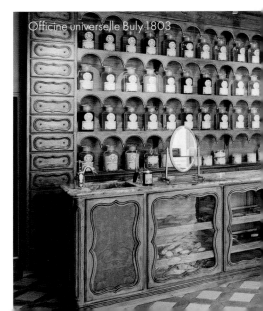

Officine universelle Buly 1803

BEAUTY AND HEALTH

Huygens

HUYGENS
GENTLE BEAUTY

In this pretty boutique in the Marais,
a new idea of beauty – natural and
tailor-made – is presented.
On one side, there are bath products with
neutral formulas to which you can add the
essential oil of your choice.
On the other side, facial treatments,
such as the best-selling gentle face scrub
that comes with a hydrating cream (19.90€).
We also love the candles, diffuser and
perfume, which should be available soon.
24, rue du Temple (4th).
M° Hôtel de Ville.
Phone: 09 83 75 70 50.
huygens.fr

HERBORIST
CHINESE BEAUTY

This giant of the Chinese beauty market
has taken its rightful place at Opéra. New
products and best sellers, such as the T'Ai Chi
mask, are sold on the first floor. Downstairs,
there are two cubicles allowing for face and
body treatments, inspired by traditional
Chinese medicine. Upstairs, a relaxing area
and teahouse are offered to V.I.P. clients.
38, avenue de l'Opéra (2nd).
M° Opéra, Quatre-Septembre.
Phone: 01 42 65 80 78.
herborist-international.com

AURÉLIE BIDERMANN
JEWELRY
DESIGNER

HER PHARMACY
LA PHARMACIE DE L'ÉPOQUE
"Vital for essential oils and
homeopathic treatments."
47-49, rue du Four (6th). M° Saint-Sulpice.
Phone: 01 45 48 53 58.
pharmaciedelepoque.fr

ESSENTIALS

EVERYONE IS SEEKING A FRAGRANCE

LIQUIDES
JUST LIKE IN A BAR

This place is just like a mojito bar,
but instead of mojitos, you are served perfume!
You just need to sit down at the counter and let
the barmaid guide you – she will ask you
questions to learn about your desires.
This is almost tailor-made, because all of the
perfumes sold here are from rare brands.
In the selection, we particularly love the Frapin
perfumes, mixed juices by Liquides
Imaginaires, and rock juices of Room 1015.
9, rue de Normandie (3rd).
M° Filles du Calvaire, Oberkampf.
Phone: 09 66 94 77 06.
liquides-parfums.com

Liquides

EX NIHILO
CUTTING EDGE OF PERFUME

This young shop brings joy to rue Saint-
Honoré with its 11 unique fragrances (prices start
at 180€ for 1 3/4 fluid ounces) and pleases fans
of tailor-made perfumes (from 290€ to 330€
for 3 1/2 fluid ounces). The Osmologue, a
beautiful, brass perfume dosing machine, mixes
"nectars" from an existing fragrance and rare,
raw materials in a heartbeat.
352, rue Saint-Honoré (1st). M° Concorde, Tuileries.
Phone: 01 40 15 93 77.
ex-nihilo-paris.com

Ex Nihilo

BORN HERE

We love the poetic and unique perfumed
items imagined by the young Parisian brand
Kerzon. Perfumed pouches for your home,
mists and candles, all made in France and
assembled in the 13th arrondissement,
delivered to Paris in 72 hours.
kerzon.fr

Nose

JOVOY
PHŒNIX

With François Hénin's passionate touch, the perfume house Jovoy is being reborn from its ashes. Jovoy is an old 1920's brand and an iconic place for small perfumeries. The boutique presents more than 150 rare fragrances. You can easily lose yourself with excitement, but, thankfully, you will be wonderfully guided through the store.

4, rue de Castiglione (1st). M° Concorde, Tuileries.
Phone: 01 40 20 06 19.
jovoyparis.com

SABÉ MASSON
EMPIRE OF THE SENSES

Welcome to the world of perfume sticks!
Sixteen designs inspire you to take on sensual gestures, like you would with a lipstick. The cosmetic line in which this brand emerged is natural, hydrating, nourishing and antioxidant (22€ for 0.18 ounce). Highly concentrated perfumes have recently started to be displayed and a line of sculpted soap is now being designed.

4, rue de Franche-Comté (3rd).
M° Filles du Calvaire, République.
Phone: 01 77 11 08 22.
sabemasson.com

NOSE
EXCLUSIVE DIAGNOSIS

In this luxurious perfumery, you can find YOUR perfume thanks to an exclusive diagnosis using 450 fragrances. If you are unsure, you can even leave with two or three samples so you can choose one later on (3€ for a sample). You will also find cosmetics with very specific properties, such as the Bioeffect treatments. This is a valuable address.

20, rue Bachaumont (2nd).
M° Sentier, Étienne Marcel.
Phone: 01 40 26 46 03.
nose.fr

Sabé Masson

FASHIONABLE **HAIR**
CUTTING EDGE HAIR SALONS

Studio Marisol

STUDIO MARISOL
LIKE AN ART GALLERY

Marisol Suarez is used to photo shoots, but she also has her own place to receive clients. This intimate space is where she creates incredible wigs that look just like an art gallery. In the living space, we love her dry haircuts that last for months and the miracle treatments she provides to hydrate dry hair and give them volume. The bonus: The famous Eric Roman comes in several days a week. Treatments start at 90€, haircuts at 100€.

33 ter, rue des Tournelles (3rd).
M° Chemin Vert, Bréguet-Sabin. Phone: 01 44 61 18 34.
studiomarisol.com

CUT BY FRED
HAIR GURU

Look for this rising star! Frédéric Birault, aka Fred, became popular through his blog and his fun and convincing hairdo tutorials. This hair guru is easy going, writes for feminine magazines, such as the beauty section of ELLE, and receives clients with an appointment in his apartment / hair salon, which is decorated with a large table, a chandelier and bargain-hunted furniture. Do you want to change your look? Haircuts start at 180€.

68, rue Hauteville (10th).
M° Poissonnière, Cadet.
Phone: 01 42 29 94 67.
cutbyfred.com

Cut By Fred

POPPY PANTONE
XXL OPENING HOURS

In her salon with retro flower tapestries on the walls, Lydiane Roger cuts dry hair — an ideal way to create a natural look, which truly pleases. We love the XXL opening hours, until 9 p.m. (except Thursdays); the 93-percent natural dyes that cover 100 percent of white hairs, the way children are welcomed and the barbershop chair in the corner. Children's haircut from 15€, women's from 55€, and beard cuts from 15€.

4, cité Dupetit-Thouars (3rd). M° Temple, République. Phone: 01 44 78 92 94.

Poppy Pantone

DJELANI MAACHI
UNDER THE MOONLIGHT

On her clients' request, Djelani Maachi cuts hair with scissors during full moons to make sure the hair will grow faster and with more volume. This werewolf hairdresser operates outside, under the moonlight, from 9 p.m. to 5 a.m. For a haircut and blow dry, prices start at 60€.

40, rue Coquillière (1st). M° Les Halles, Louvre-Rivoli. Phone: 01 42 33 57 47.

EVERYONE LOOKS FOR THE RIGHT CUT (ONLINE)

On Haircvt, you can swipe through haircuts to choose the hairdresser whose work will suit you best. Among the 220 professionals on the website, you can refine your search according to different criteria, such as the neighborhood or the price. The bonuses? The online appointment service and payment at the time of the appointment.
haircvt.fr

DAVID LUCAS
OUR FAVORITE

He is the all-time favorite hairdresser of the ELLE editorial board. David receives his clients in his Haussman-style salon/apartment that looks like an art gallery. His cuts and dyes make you look younger and service starts at 8:30 a.m. What a great way to start the day! For semi-long hair, the cut and hairdo starts at 102€. The bonus: His own line of hair products free of sulfate, paraben, coloring and silicon for the shampoo.

20, rue Danielle-Casanova (2nd). M° Pyramides, Opéra. Phone: 01 47 03 92 04.

BY ELINA
TAILOR-MADE

This is the place where you will find your shade, the one and only that no one will even notice, because it will look so natural! Elina and her team with the magical touch provide only tailor-made services. The bonuses: The best blow dries in Paris and perfect opening hours for working girls, from Monday to Saturday, 9 a.m. to 9 p.m.

14, rue du Champ-de-Mars (7th). M° École Militaire. Phone: 01 45 51 26 51. byelina.com

BE **SPORTY!**
THE BEST GYMS TO GET GOING!

LA MAISON POPINCOURT
AQUA CYCLING ++

This aqua cycling gym looks like a spa.
Come pedal in a 45-minute session with a
seasoned coach in a huge pool underneath a
glass roof. Thighs, abs, and booty: it is a full
workout! No need for you to bring a towel and
flip-flops – the Maison provides everything.
You can also book sessions of Dôme lyashi, an
individual Japanese sauna to sweat and relax.
A ten-session plan costs 260€.
16, rue de Verneuil (7th).
M° Saint-Germain-des-Prés, Rue du Bac.
Phone: 01 42 60 48 59.
lamaisonpopincourt.com

La Maison Popincourt

Studio Harmonic

STUDIO HARMONIC
DANCING STUDIO

Contemporary, Bollywood, salsa, flamenco,
the Studio Harmonic may be lesser known than
the Centre du Marais, but it is just as good.
The rooms are luminous, there is a snacking
space to regain strength after your workout,
and the prices are appealing – this studio has
a lot going for it! Wayne Byars' ground bar
courses are effective and fun, and particularly
popular among Opera dancers and stars.
A course is 17€, and the studio offers plans with
prices on a sliding scale.
5, passage des Taillandiers (11th). M° Bastille,
Ledru-Rollin. Phone: 01 48 07 13 39.
studioharmonic.fr

QEE
IN FRESH AIR

This wellness center offers a full program: alternative medicine consultations, pilates and yoga lessons in spacious rooms. When the weather allows it, courses take place outdoors in the courtyard. The organic and vegan restaurant next to the center provides a nice finish to your health session! It is located next to numerous offices, so it can be busy at lunchtime.

Main address: 39, rue de Châteaudun (9th).
M° Notre-Dame-de-Lorette.
Phone: 01 40 16 08 00.
Annex: 4, rue Camille-Tahan (18th).
M° La Fourche, Place de Clichy.
Phone: 01 40 16 08 00.
qee.fr

LET'S RIDE
INDOOR CYCLING

To stay fit, the latest trend is indoor cycling. In intended darkness and an electric atmosphere, riders pedal 45 minutes at varying speeds and with music. They promise a full body workout. The first two sessions cost 25€, then the prices vary between 25 and 16€ per session, depending on the number you buy.
21, rue des Trois-Bornes (11th).
M° Oberkampf, Parmentier.
Phone: 01 84 05 81 91.
letsride.fr

PRIVATE LESSONS

· With Spearit, you can book an appointment via instant messaging, phone call or text message with the right instructor in dozens of fields. You can choose the instructor by looking at their page, which includes photos, information on their practice, pricing, hours, etc. Private or semi-private lessons with up to six participants.
spearit.co

· On Train Me, a team approves each coach, and the latter has a presentation page with a real-time updated calendar of his/her availability. Before booking, you can send the chosen coach a message. He or she will respond within 24 hours to make a first contact and determine a place to have the lessons. Lessons are solo or in a small group of up to four people.
trainme.co

Let's ride

PASS SPORT

A great idea by Somuchmore and Try&Do, this monthly pass provides access to hundreds of Parisian gyms, at an incredible price! Once you are a member, their website becomes a great booking platform for thousands of lessons. From 39€ for four lessons to 89€ unlimited per month on somuchmore.fr ; from 49€ (four lessons) to 99€ (unlimited) per month on tryndo.com

LA BELLE ĒQUIPE
SOLO OR WITH OTHERS

Here, you can learn the basics of Thaï boxing (muay thai), Brazilian jiu-jitsu or yoga, and you will be guided so that you can achieve your sporting goals. Take collective lessons that welcome up to sixteen people or private lessons in a courtyard building classified as a Historic Monument. Book single lessons (225€ for ten semi-private lessons) or a monthly plan (starts at 150€).

14, rue d'Abbeville (10th). M° Poissonnière, Gare du Nord. Phone: 09 81 99 06 60. labelleequipeparis.fr

SIGOLĒNE PRĒBOIS
DESIGNER AND FOUNDER OF TSĒ & TSĒ

HER CYCLING GYM
CYCLOFFICINE

"A cooperative bike reparation studio where you can learn to repair your bike. Do it yourself is just the right spirit for Tsé & Tsé. To repair, preserve, improve and upcycle are actions that mean a lot to me."

15, rue Pierre-Bonnard (20th). M° Gambetta, Porte de Bagnolet. Phone: 09 72 35 93 12. www.cyclocoop.org

AQUA BY
JUMP IN THE WATER!

This aqua cycling gym does everything right. Ninety-six lessons take place every week with eight different coaches giving varied and lively lessons. There is a chic pool that fits up to fifteen bikes, two locker rooms, a spa with a swimsuit dryer and that also offers make-up remover and hair straighteners. After your workout, you can go to the sauna to prevent sore muscles the next day! Opt for the yearly plan or use free booking (300€ for ten sessions, starting at 79€ for four sessions a month).

82, rue Notre-Dame-de-Nazareth (3rd) M° Strasbourg Saint-Denis. Phone: 01 44 61 74 01. aqua-by.com

Aqua By

Ken Club

Front de Seine

FRONT DE SEINE
THE PERFECT GYM?

This is the gym you dream of having next to your apartment. Front de Seine is one of the few places where you can play squash in Paris, with four beautiful rooms. Coaches will take care of you and monitor your progress during private sessions. Lessons start at 10€ with a maximum attendance of seven people.
Two apps let you follow the evolution of your body. The machines are all connected and you can have a drink after your workout at a real bar with an outside seating area.
When do we start?
44, rue Emeriau (15th). M° Charles Michel.
Phone: 01 45 75 35 37. frontdeseine.net

LUXURY OR LOW COST?

· On one hand, three high-end gyms present chic designs, state-of-the-art machines and in-depth courses: the famous Ken Club (100, avenue du Président-Kennedy, 16th. RER Avenue du Président Kennedy.), two Parisian gyms L'Usine (in the 2nd et 4th, on usineopera.com), and Le Klay, which features an amazing restaurant with a glass roof near the entrance (4 bis, rue Saint-Sauveur, 2nd. M° Réaumur-Sébastopol.).
Day plans allow you to discover these places. Otherwise, prices range from 1,800€ to 3,400€ for a year.
· On the other hand, some gyms offer low-cost plans on off-peak times, morning plans or even unlimited plans with an all-machine and all-courses access. The champion of these gyms is Neoness (nine Parisian addresses on neoness-forme.com), closely followed by Fitness Price, which offers many options (six addresses on fitnessprice.com).
Prices range from 10€ to 39.90€ a month.

BEST OF **YOGA**

ESSENTIAL CLUBS,
NEW SPACES AND SPECIALTY STORES

Rasa Yoga

RASA YOGA
COMPLETE AND BILINGUAL

Daniela Schmid is an architect and a passionate yogi. She designed a refined studio with a welcoming space, two rooms for practice and a massage room. Each week, well-trained instructors give nearly eighty lessons at all levels , in French and in English. In 2005 Daniela opened the first multi-practice yoga studio: Haltha Flow, Ashtanga, Lyengar, Vinyasa, Yin, Kundalini, etc.

21, rue Saint-Jacques (5th).
M° Cluny-La Sorbonne, Saint-Michel.
Phone: 01 43 54 14 59.
rasa-yogarivegauche.com

ASHTANGA YOGA PARIS
ULTRA DYNAMIC

This is an iconic place for traditional Ashtanga practice in Paris, open to beginners and seasoned yogis. The studio opens at 6:30 a.m. for people who want to practice Mysore freely. Courses to practice Ashtanga, Vinyasa (a dynamic approach that stems from Ashtanga), restorative Yin (soft and a good complement), and Pranayama (breathing exercises) training follow all day long.

40, avenue de la République (11th).
M° Parmentier.
Phone: 01 45 80 19 96.
ashtangayogaparis.fr

Ashtanga Yoga Paris

CAELO YOGA
FAMILY PRACTICE

Hidden behind a courtyard, the yoga center welcomes seasoned yogis, children, pregnant women and beginners with its new Beginner Series plan: four lessons to discover different types of yoga, and two courses to acquire the basic postures (99€). Forty-five lessons take place each week to practice Jivamukti, Vinyasa, Yin, etc. The first month costs 119€, then 149€ a month in the six-month plan.

55, rue Montmartre (2nd). M° Sentier, Étienne Marcel.
Phone: 01 45 08 59 10.
caeloyoga.com

YOGA COLIBRI
DYNAMIC ZEN

At the heart of Le Sentier, Eric Depoil's studio favors Ashtanga – a dynamic type of yoga. The large room can welcome up to forty people and opens at 7 a.m. with the Mysore. At lunchtime and in the evening, he teaches 90-minute Ashtanga lessons. At lunchtime on Thursdays, Jivamukti is taught. On weekends, courses in Yin and Restorative offer a smooth workout.

7, rue Notre-Dame-de-Bonne-Nouvelle (2nd).
M° Bonne Nouvelle, Strasbourg Saint-Denis.
Phone: 01 75 50 07 14. yoga-colibri.com

Caelo Yoga

Gérard Arnaud Yoga

GÉRARD ARNAUD YOGA
SMOOTH

In two studios in the 11th, you can practice Vinyasa yoga that is altogether dynamic, creative, soft and smooth for your body, following the method created by Gérard Arnaud. Nearly fifteen classes take place each day, including recovery courses: Relaxation, Yin, Meditation Flow or Nidra Yoga.

3, passage Rauch (11th). M° Charonne, Ledru-Rollin.
11, passage Saint-Pierre-Amelot (11th).
M° Oberkampf, Filles du Calvaire.
Phone: 01 47 00 26 12.
yoga-paris.com

Le Tigre Yoga

YOGA SEARCHER
ALL OVER THE PLACE

Behind this brand name, there are several places of yoga (and surfing) retreats, a clothing brand for training (but not only) and a Parisian concept store. On the first floor, clothing lines are displayed next to organic herbal teas, cold-pressed juices and slow cosmetics. Downstairs, you can register to practice Anusara, Vinyasa or Yin.

53, boulevard Beaumarchais (3rd).
M° Chemin Vert, Bréguet-Sabin.
yogasearcher.com

Yoga Searcher

FOUR ESSENTIAL SPOTS

· Le Tigre Yoga welcomes adults and children to its two Parisian studios, which have excellent instructors and regular workshops. 250€ for ten lessons (in both studios), 1,950€ for yearly unlimited access.

101, rue du Cherche-Midi (7th).
M° Duroc, Falguière. Phone: 01 58 80 06 06.
17-19, rue de Chaillot (16th). M° Iéna, Alma-Marceau.
Phone: 09 84 54 17 34.
tigre-yoga.com

· Beyoga: In this studio hidden in a small pathway, all types of yogas are taught, from the essential Ashtanga to the surprising Yogaplates (a mixture of yoga and Pilates). 22€ for a lesson, 125€ for six lessons.

17, rue Campagne-Première (14th).
M° Raspail, RER Port-Royal.
Phone: 01 40 47 67 63 and 09 65 31 60 11.

· Yoga Village Paris is a smooth yoga haven close to Madeleine. Different types of yoga are taught all day long, as well as pilates. 22€ for a lesson, 60€ for three.

39, boulevard des Capucines (2nd).
M° Opéra, Madeleine.
Phone: 01 72 34 58 47.
yogavillage.fr

· Yoga Iyengar 91 is made up of two large rooms around a courtyard garden, where Iyengar is taught. It is the most precise type of yoga. 25€ for a lesson, 200€ for ten, 350€ for twenty, and 450€ for thirty.

91, rue du Faubourg-Saint-Martin (10th).
M° Château d'Eau, Jacques Bonsergent.
yoga-iyengar91.com

YOGA CONCEPT
CLOTHES AND MATS

A pioneer in Paris, Pamela Lévy has gathered together American, European and French brands in her small store in the Marais. Her motto: "Technique, style, ethics and good advice". The clothes must fit the exercise. Even men find what they are looking for here. Better yet, she formed partnerships with French brands to design exclusive accessories.

123, rue de Turenne (3rd). M° Filles du Calvaire.
Phone: 01 42 77 74 67.

yogaconcept.com

Mirz Yoga

Yoga Concept

LOLË
HIGH-END

This Canadian brand combines a line of clothing and specific accessories as well as numerous lessons. On the fourth floor of the Galeries Lafayette Haussmann, the studio offers up to five classes a day. Training sessions are organized at the Atelier du Marais too. Facebook check-in mandatory.

9, rue des Blancs-Manteaux (4th).
M° Saint-Paul, Hôtel de Ville. Phone: 01 42 78 18 24.

MIRZ YOGA
GROOVE

This is both a brand for mixed clothing and a studio, located on the bottom floor of a former nineteenth-century printer. Marine Parmentier teaches Hatha Yoga, as well as a yoga-based R&B that consists of Hatha poses set to a lively rhythm. She invites many instructors. The schedule includes forty lessons a week. Themed workshops that focus on food, health and lifestyle issues take place on Sundays. Nurturing!

6, rue Arthur-Rozier (19th).
M° Place des Fêtes.

mirz-yoga.com

THE BIG
BLUE

TRENDIEST POOLS. JUMP IN!

Molitor

ESPACE SPORTIF PAILLERON
FROM 7 TO 77 YEARS OLD

Here is the most kid-friendly pool in Paris!
It is hidden inside a sports center managed by
the UCPA, which includes a gym and an ice-
skating rink (closed in July and August).
Parents and children can enjoy the sports pool,
Jacuzzi, kids' pool and outdoor lawn in the
summer. Entrance: 3.60€.

32, rue Édouard-Pailleron (19th). M° Bolivar, Jaurès.
Phone: 01 40 40 27 70.

paulleron19.com

MOLITOR
LUXURIOUS

This iconic pool is part of a luxurious hotel,
but anyone can access it! For 55€, the Early
Swim plan provides 1 hour of swimming,
followed by a filling breakfast, from 7 to
9:30 a.m. For those of you who are not early
birds, the Swim & Lunch, Swim & Dinner and
Swim & Drunch plans are just as sexy,
although pricier (starting at 79€).

13, rue Nungesser-et-Coli (16th).
M° Porte d'Auteuil.
Phone: 01 56 07 08 50.
mltr.fr

Espace sportif Pailleron

ALL YOU NEED

Paris Piscines is an app available
on the App Store and Google Play
that provides all the information
you need on Parisian pools.
You can even chat with others
about unusual closing times or
rush hours.

BUTTE AUX CAILLES
THE ANCESTOR

This is one of the oldest pools in Paris and has recently been entirely remade. You can still swim in 82 degrees Fahrenheit spring water that comes directly from the basement, thanks to a pressure system. Now you can even enjoy this all year long (except when the weather is bad) in the indoor pool, underneath an Art deco arch, or in the outdoors rooftop pool. Prices are the same as in all of the other town pools: 3€ for a single entrance, 24€ for ten.

5, place Paul-Verlaine (13th). M° Tolbiac, Corvisart. Phone: 01 45 89 60 05.

DELPHINE PLISSON
FOUNDER OF MAISON PLISSON

HER POOL
PISCINE JOSÉPHINE-BAKER

"This is a wonderful town pool located on the banks of the Seine, where you can swim by the river and in the sun during summer! I sometimes go there on my lunch break."

Quai François-Mauriac (13th).
M° Quai de la Gare.
Phone: 01 56 61 96 50.

SUZANNE BERLIOUX
AT THE HEART OF PARIS

Ideally located, this 164-foot pool welcomes all kinds of aquatic activities; a special lane is reserved for fin swimming, aqua cycling, swimming lessons. During the week, you can go there until 9:15 p.m. or 10:15 p.m. Entrance: 4.80€.

10, place de la Rotonde (1st). RER Châtelet-Les Halles, M° Les Halles. Phone: 01 42 36 36 82.

piscine-halles@carilis.fr

HOME DECOR

A PARISIAN WOMAN NEEDS TO **FEEL GOOD** IN HER OWN HOME !

HOME
SPIRIT
PRETTY STORES TO SPRUCE UP YOUR INTERIOR

Le Petit Désordre

LE PETIT DÉSORDRE
NORTHERN INSPIRATION

This Petit Désordre is close to the accessory store Désordre Urbain. It features decor objects and furniture, with a north-inspired selection: tables and an ingenious desk/console table by Danish brand Hübsch; stationery; baskets made from plastic cords; Portuguese soap; graphic silicone place mats, etc. Whip out your credit card!

94, rue Nollet (17th). M° Brochant.
Phone: 01 46 27 62 93.

BORGO DELLE TOVAGLIE
FOR APARTMENTS

This 837-square-yard old rubber factory, decorated like an apartment, holds everything you will need for your home. Lenin drapes, retro tableware, and pompom cushions, the objects range from simple to kitsch. The real plus at Italian-born Borgo's is the bistro on the patio, where you can taste and buy excellent specialties from beyond the Alps.

4, rue du Grand-Prieuré (11th).
M° Oberkampf.
Phone: 09 82 33 64 81.

MADELEINE & GUSTAVE
CAKE INCLUDED

After trying out his business in a store on Ile-d'Yeu, Pascale Gibert decided to go big in the City of Lights, with a beautiful 478-square-yard space dispatched on three levels. A north-inspired decor where white and ceramic tableware mix, along with table linens, lamps and rope carpets, etc. Recently, she launched a homemade brand of house linen. Upstairs, you will find a coffee shop where you can relax and enjoy a piece of cake.

19, rue Yves-Toudic (10th). M° Jacques Bonsergent,
République. Phone: 01 40 38 61 02.
madeleine-gustave.com

COLONEL
FRENCH DESIGN

The spirit of being on a vacation is captured in the design duo Isabelle Gilles and Yann Poncelet's creations. We love the fresh blond wood furniture, the Faces lamp with its tilting lampshade – and all is made in France.

14, avenue Richerand (10th).
M° Goncourt.
Phone: 01 83 89 69 22.
moncolonel.fr

JULIETTE LĒVY
FOUNDER OF THE STORE
OH MY CREAM!

HER DECOR STORE
CARAVANE

"It's simple: Here, I want to buy everything! I adore their collection, which mixes bohemian style with a touch of chic."
Four stores (4th, 6th and 12th)
and a corner in Bon Marché (7th).
caravane.fr

MAISON M
MAGAZINE HOME

Caroline Tossan-Cavillard is a lifestyle journalist who reinvented herself as a home decorator. Contemporary furniture, candles, tableware, lamps, in her store everything is put together as in a picture from a magazine.
25, rue de Bourgogne (7th). M° Varenne, Assemblée Nationale. Phone: 01 47 53 07 74.
maisonmparis.com

Maison M

PERNETY MĒNAGER
DIY AND SHARING

Suppliers of hardware and other products for the home, all in all Pernety Ménager is a tiny version of the BHV basement. As a bonus, it provides ideas for gifts that range from bento boxes to the smart spread knife that heats up when handled. Of course, housekeeping products are also sold here, and good advice is given.
83, rue Raymond-Losserand (14th). M° Pernety.
Phone: 01 45 42 59 23.

Madeleine & Gustave

Liberty's

LIBERTY'S
TOP BOUTIQUE
You cannot miss this genuine neighborhood location! Marie-Louise Dilla's shop overflows onto the sidewalk of rue Oberkampf and welcomes regular customers. This boutique is small, long and narrow, but it is full of Berber rugs, drapes, cushions and bath towels in elegant tones and padded and colorful bedspreads. A very chic mini souk, with surprisingly good prices.
75, rue Oberkampf (11th).
M° Parmentier.
Phone: 01 43 38 04 24.

RED EDITION
NEO-1950'S
This brand's secret place is an apartment where neo-1950's furniture is displayed in a home-like setting: chairs, couches and tables. Everything comes from a designer collective, and everything is well made: furniture lacquered in quirky colors, an Ellipse mirror in a displaced circle, a copper-wood openwork panel – we will say no more!
38, rue des Blancs-Manteaux (4th).
M° Rambuteau, Hôtel de Ville.
Plan a visit by calling 01 43 37 02 87.
rededition.com

MOVE OUT
JUM offers professional moving services on his website. He can move all kinds of furniture, except pianos (pricing starts at 37€).
get-jum.com

Red Edition

Laurette

LAURETTE
FOR ALL AGES
Specializers in children's furniture,
the brand Laurette also offers some adult
furniture in the line "Ligne L" (bed, desk,
bedside table). We love the vintage style,
the wood taken from eco-friendly forests and
the choice of dozens of different colors.
18, rue Mabillon (6th).
M° Mabillon, Saint-Sulpice.
Phone: 01 46 34 35 22.
laurette-deco.com

Blou

BLOU
KINGS OF THE 17TH
Blou started with a store at number 77
of rue Legendre, which expanded to
number 75, and it recently opened a third
boutique at 20, rue des Dames — it is invading
the 17th! In the first two locations, you will find
hipster furniture, decor accessories and men's
fashion. In the third location, the Danish brand
Hay is featured ; everything here is designed
with intelligence, from notebooks to couches.
75, rue Legendre (17th). M° Brochant, La Fourche.
Phone: 09 53 04 67 53.
77, rue Legendre (17th). M° Brochant, La Fourche.
Phone: 01 46 27 50 84.
blou-paris.fr

KANN DESIGN
RIGHTFULLY CHIC
This architect and designer collective
creates tables and bookcases in recycled
wood, 1950's-style dressers and Scandinavian
coffee tables. Kann Design also showcases
other decor brands: functionals lamps,
Rouge du Rhin cushions, etc.
28, rue des Vinaigriers (10th).
M° Jacques Bonsergent, Gare de l'Est.
Phone: 09 53 40 86 98.
8, rue des Moines (17th). M° Brochant.
Phone: 09 51 64 50 13.
kanndesign.com

Kann Design

Poetic in Rock

POETIC IN ROCK
STRIPPED-DOWN STYLE

**Pascale Portella is a home stylist
in a poetic rock style.** She does interior
design and displays her selection of
objects from around the world in her
showroom/store, along with her own
textile creations. We love her style,
which mixes bohemian and stripped-down
looks – it can easily rock an interior!
This bohemian-chic gold mine, hidden
in a quiet street of the 7th, features waxed
concrete ceiling lights, big round
cushions and small mattresses she
designs herself, as well as sheepskin chairs.
1, rue Saint-Simon (7th).
M° Rue du Bac.
Phone: 01 45 44 01 73 and 06 30 49 76 52.
poetic-in-rock.com

STORIE
BRITISH STYLE

The ethnic-chic environment of this store
is where Fiona (originally from England),
presents objects that tell a story. Her
selection is fair and eco-friendly, but it is also
stylish. We love the wooden radios, graphic
rugs made from woven plastic, baskets made
from telephone cords, bamboo ceiling lights,
as well as her selection of bohemian jewellery.
And we love her warm welcome.
20, rue Delambre (14th).
M° Vavin, Edgar Quinet.
Phone: 01 83 56 01 98.
storieshop.com

CHEZ MOI, PARIS
MAN, SWEET MAN

Chez moi is at Jean-Baptise Charpenay-Limon's place. It is a real apartment where this young man lives. He changes the decor every three months. His sharp selection of young designer objects and bargain-hunted items is for sale: his bed, tableware, his bookcase and even his books. Everything must go — except him!

25, rue Hérold (1ʳ). M° Étienne Marcel, Sentier.
Phone: 06 61 26 23 31.
chezmoiparis.com

ALETH VIGNON
RARE OBJECTS

Aleth Vignon selects objects you will not see everywhere: tableware, rugs, small furniture, lamps. Her favorite brands include Linge Particulier, which makes washed linen in unprecedented colors. Here, you can order the most beautiful custom-made (and expensive) blinds, drapes and sliding doors in Paris.

87, rue Lemercier (17ᵗʰ). M° Brochant, La Fourche.
Phone: 01 42 63 75 40.
alethvignon.com

LAB.
ALL AGES

Elodie Laleous created her own brand of home linens for babies and adults. You can go there to find washed linen sheets and tablecloths, Liberty cushions and made-in-France items — and enjoy the mixture of bright colors and soft tones. Her smart idea? She created a cushion bar so customers can make their own selection.

10, rue Notre-Dame-de-Lorette (9ᵗʰ).
M° Saint-Georges, Notre-Dame-de-Lorette.
Phone: 01 71 39 54 82. lab-boutique.com

SMALL **DECOR**
PLACES WITH NICE KNICK-KNACKS AND CHARMING PRESENTS

LES FLEURS
FAVORITE

In this beautiful space, where everything is arranged tastefully, we want to buy everything – small decor, bargain-hunted furniture, tableware, stationery, plants! Items are designed by young talents or famous brands, and pricing is accessible. Do not miss their affordable "gift-jewelry-accessory" store a few streets away.

5, rue Trousseau (11th).
M° Ledru-Rollin, Faidherbe-Chaligny.
Phone: 01 43 55 12 94.
6, passage Josset (11th).
M° Ledru-Rollin, Bastille.
Phone: 01 43 55 12 94.
boutiquelesfleurs.com

LA MANUFACTURE PARISIENNE
CONFIDENTIAL PARIS

This store and publisher, which is located near the Jules Joffrin metro station, changes its selection each month, choosing a different theme and mixing furniture and items of home decor. Herveline Fabre designs her own made-in-France line, and finds truly confidential designers.

93, rue Marcadet (18th).
M° Jules Joffrin, Marcadet-Poissonniers.
Phone: 01 42 64 76 29.
lamanufactureparisienne.fr

THE KEY ANGEL

Keyper keeps copies of your keys safe: the keys to your house, car, scooter, desk and wine cellar. You register online and receive a Keyperbox to put your extra key in, seal it and send it back. When you need it urgently, because you lost your keys or they were stolen, a delivery person arrives within an hour to hand you the extra key (prices start at 24.90€ for a delivery +3.90€ per month or 39.90€ for a year).
keyper.fr

Maison Aimable

MAISON AIMABLE
HALF ETHNIC, HALF NORDIC
This store contains a great variety of ideas for presents. Graphic notebooks, pill boxes, tableware, lamps, rugs and mirrors, the selection is refined and affordable, and the style mixes ethnic and Nordic.
16-18, rue des Taillandiers (11th).
M° Bastille, Ledru-Rollin.
Phone: 09 82 53 16 18.
maison-aimable.com

Philippe Model Maison

L'ATELIER DE PABLO
PRETTY JUNK ROOM
To find a present at the last minute, head toward this pretty catch-all store, where small furniture, lamps, tableware, toys, scarves and new and vintage gadgets are displayed. It is full of cheap knick-knacks starting at 2€. It even includes producer priced wine and champagne!
34, rue d'Hauteville (10th). M° Bonne Nouvelle, Château d'Eau. Phone: 01 47 70 21 29.
latelierdepablo.com

L'Atelier de Pablo

PHILIPPE MODEL MAISON
CHROMATIC COMEDY
Everything must be colorful is the only rule here. Philippe Model works both in fashion and home styling, and he displays his own designs along with his friends'. Everything harmonizes well and reflects his search for nice tones, from the beautiful Peruvian alpaca rug to the bistro chairs with motifs. A few steps away, at number 69 of the same street, his sneaker store is also worth a look!
65, rue Condorcet (9th). M° Saint-Georges, Pigalle.
Phone: 01 48 03 92 58.

JAMINI
CHIC AND FAIR TRADE

The made-in-India rugs, cushions, scarves and clutches that you will find here are all hand-woven in beautiful cotton, wool and silk, printed with stamps. Everything is fair trade and chic, even the project of the creator Usha Bora, who raises awareness on animal poaching and deforestation by selling pretty notebooks made from rhino and elephant faces.

10, rue Notre-Dame-de-Lorette (9th).
M° Notre-Dame-de-Lorette, Saint-Georges.
Phone: 09 83 88 91 06.
10, rue du Château d'Eau (10th). M° Jacques Bonsergent, République. Phone: 09 82 34 78 53.
jaminidesign.com

BAZARTHERAPY
HAPPY BAZAAR!

This place was designed as a grocery store for objects, and satisfies your every need, from the 3€ gadget to the 2,000€ extensible table. This bazaar also has its own table designer with almost custom-made formats and styles.

15, rue Beaurepaire (10th). M° Jacques Bonsergent, République. Phone: 01 42 40 10 11.
bazartherapy.com

LA TRÉSORERIE
USEFUL THINGS

Inspired by old-time hardware and notions stores where you could find all the small household equipment you needed, La Trésorerie gathers together beautiful objects and products that are useful and respectful of the environment, with 90 percent made in Europe and at accessible pricing.

11, rue du Château d'Eau (10th). M° Jacques Bonsergent, République. Phone: 01 40 40 20 46.
latresorerie.fr

Jamini

La Trésorerie

OMY
LIKE AN IMAGE
Omy coloring items are super fun,
and they are for children and adults alike.
Place mats, huge coloring posters,
"pocket maps" for popular traveling
destinations, birthday packs and washable
permanent markers can be found here.
2, rue Gabriel-Laumain (10th). M° Bonne Nouvelle,
Château d'Eau. Phone: 01 48 00 18 49.
omy.fr

Papier Tigre

CAMILLE GOUTAL
PERFUMER
AT MAISON
ANNICK GOUTAL

HER DECOR STORE
FLEUX'
"These four decor stores are great
places to find accessories and
furniture, but also small gifts and
quirky items. They are for all tastes
and all budgets!"
39 and 52, rue Sainte-Croix-de-la-Bretonnerie (4th). M° Hôtel de Ville.
Phone: 01 42 78 27 20.
fleux.com

PAPIER TIGRE
100-PERCENT FRENCH
At this fun place, you will discover
notebooks, boxes, labels and wall storage,
all inspired by origami. These designer
creations are also almost 100 percent made in
France, and the cardboard used is recycled.
Other French-made products sold here include
Le Baigneur soap and Kerzon candles.
5, rue des Filles-du-Calvaire (3th).
M° Filles du Calvaire, Saint-Sébastien Froissart.
Phone: 01 48 04 00 21.
papiertigre.fr

Pop Market

POP MARKET
SUPERSONIC

In this rock'n'roll concept store managed by Céline Fischetti, you can find fun gifts: ringing wallets, Macon&Lesquoy embroidered broaches, computer pouches that look like kraft envelopes. This is a must-go place right before Christmas.

50, rue Bichat (10th).
M° Jacques Bonsergent,
M° and RER Gare de l'Est.
Phone: 09 52 79 96 86.
popmarket.frw

ASTIER DE VILLATTE
BLACK AND WHITE

This place is famous for its beautiful ceramics made from black earthenware with white glaze, its luxurious perfumed items (Cologne, skin treatments, incense and candles), and its stationery. You must go to the quirky store in the 1st, which offers an exceptional journey into old-time Paris.

173, rue Saint-Honoré (1st).
M° Palais Royal-Musée du Louvre, Pyramides.
Phone: 01 42 60 74 13.
16, rue de Tournon (6th). M° Odéon, RER Luxembourg.
Phone: 01 42 03 43 90.
astierdevillatte.com

LES SAINTES CHÈRIES
FAVORITE

Across the road from the Saint-Martin market, Marjorie opened two stores, where she displays popular decor accessories. The designs are contemporary, the prices affordable and everything is made in France or handmade. Next to the store, the small Saintes Chéries Café offers tarts, fruit and vegetable juices.

29 and 41, rue Bouchardon (10th). M° Château d'Eau, Jacques Bonsergent. Phone: 01 42 03 42 56.

Astier de Villatte

ANNEXE
POP POP POP UP

Sessùn, the brand from Marseille,
has recently opened a pop-up store right next to its fashion boutique. You can find personal favorites and pop-up collections here.
The line changes every three months and is organized by theme: sea, dance hall, London, cold weather.
32, rue de Charonne (11th). M° Ledru-Rollin, Bastille.
Phone: 01 48 07 18 26.
sessun.fr

LE ROCKETSHIP
MULTITASK

Benoît Touche is passionate about graphic design, photography and coffee. At first, he struggled to decide which passion to favor. In the end, he decided to combine them all. Le Rocketship gathers well thought-out decor items in limited series, along with homemade designs such as Benoit's photographs and the illustrated posters by his brother, Misteratomic. He also serves coffee made with a state-of-the-art coffee machine.
13 bis, rue Henry-Monnier (9th).
M° Pigalle, Saint-Georges. Phone: 01 48 78 23 66.
lerocketship.com

Annexe

Le Rocketship

PAR L'OBJET
AFFORDABLE!

The store is small, but its unicolor and well-designed windows catch the eye. Inside, Marianne makes it her mission to feature only affordable designer items: candles, vases, jewelry, rugs, bags and small furniture.
This selection will encourage you to get a lot of gifts for everyone!
103, rue Caulaincourt (18th). M° Lamarck-Caulaincourt.
Phone: 01 44 92 09 34.

BARGAIN
HUNT
SMART PLACES TO FIND GEMS

Ā DEMAIN...
DESIGN-ONLY.COM
SECOND-HAND SHOP / GALLERY

This place gathers home design items from the 1950's to the 80's! Great designer pieces (Jacobsen, Saarinen, Paulin) are mixed with unsigned furniture, small and inexpensive items you will fall in love with, and vintage clothes on a rack that evolves with new arrivals. The novice collector will enjoy this mixture of gallery and second-hand shop without spending too much.

97, rue de Turenne (3rd).
M° Filles du Calvaire, Saint-Sébastien Froissart.
Phone: 09 81 97 70 06.
design-only.com

A demain... design-only.com

NATSUMI ET JĒRŌME
SEVENTH HEAVEN

This popular second-hand shop is somewhat incongruous in the very chic 7th arrondissement. In this joyous setting, bric-a-brac, kitchen furniture and numerous accessories used in country houses from the 1900's to the 60's are sold, bargain hunted and repaired. There is a particularly large choice of lamps. Note that this boutique is open only in the afternoons.

15, boulevard de la Tour-Maubourg (7th). M° Invalides, La Tour-Maubourg. Phone: 09 80 37 33 79.
brocantenatsumietjerome.wordpress.com

LES ULTIMES
TOTALLY FIFTIES

Another 1950's second-hand shop!
Les Ultimes has new arrivals every fifteen days. It displays sideboards, teak coffee tables with Dutch chairs, bedside tables, along with folded metal frame holders and shelves. These smart designs exist in different colors, and can be custom-made.

5, rue Antoine-Vollon (12th).
M° Ledru-Rollin.
Phone: 09 50 92 93 89.
lesultimes.com

DALLAS, NORMANDIE
CABINET OF CURIOSITIES

This pretty second-hand shop displays objects and furniture from the 1930's to the 80's. A mailman locker, teak coffee table, kitsch and offbeat tableware. And let's not forget the collection of chairs, entirely reupholstered by the brand Bloc de l'Est, and that takes us back to the Soviet style of the 50's!

13, rue Réaumur (3th). M° Arts et Métiers, Temple.
Phone: 06 65 70 13 10.
dallasnormandie.com

BARGAIN HUNT FOR A TREASURE

On the website or the app, Brocabrac lists all the garage sales and flea markets happening near you. All you need to do is enter your postcode (like a zip code), and a list of dates will appear along with a list of the cities and regions near you, the number of participants and the organizer's contact. This is an essential tool for bargain hunters!
brocabrac.fr

MOBILHOME
BEAUTIFUL AND CHEAP

In this large store, Pascale accomplishes her vintage dreams by displaying 1960's couches, English extension tables and Scandinavian sideboards with secret drawers. She loves furniture with surprises. She also sells her own lamps in the Jean Prouvé style, but much cheaper!

108, rue Legendre (17th).
M° Brochant, La Fourche.
Phone: 01 58 59 10 01.
chezmobilhome.com

Mobilhome

Tombées du Camion

TOMBÉES DU CAMION
COOL KNICK-KNACKS

This atypical pocket-size store
pays homage to old, useless and ordinary
objects. Even the walls and ceiling are
covered with numerous little things found in
abandoned factory stocks, old lots and notions
collections. By searching through them,
you can find old glass pharmacy flasks,
toy soldiers, bar tokens and, more surprising,
objects such as martinets, moustache noses
and even keys. Everything is sold from
1€ to 5€.

17, rue Joseph-de-Maistre (18th).
M° Abbesses, Blanche.
tombeesducamion.com

« OBJET DIRECT »
ATTACK

In this small 215-square-foot store, a precise
selection of furniture from all time periods is
displayed, in a good state and at the right
price, chosen from the heart. Be careful:
The boutique is open only from Thursdays to
Saturdays, and it is very busy. Everything is sold
within two days, with a single restocking on
Saturdays. As the manager Emmanuel says:
"Things need to flow!"

365, rue des Pyrénées (20th). M° Jourdain, Pyrénées.
Phone: 01 47 97 61 19.

THE FLEA MARKET AT CARRÉ POPINCOURT

People come to shop for second-hands in this village-like area of the 11th. If you are looking for small Parisian or Scandinavian furniture, you have a vast choice at the three places of the Marché-Popincourt. Even the sellers at the Saint-Ouen flea market bargain hunt here!

· Alasinglinglin : 14, rue Ternaux (11th).
M° Parmentier, Oberkampf.
Phone: 01 43 38 45 54.
· Trolls et Puces : 3, rue du Marché-Popincourt (11th).
M° Parmentier, Oberkampf.
Phone: 01 43 14 60 00.
· Belle Lurette : 5, rue du Marché-Popincourt (11th).
M° Parmentier, Oberkampf.
Phone: 01 43 38 67 39.

AU GRAND MAGASIN
NOSTALGIC CHIC

This new second-hand shop in the 11th is filled with small retro wonders: old toys, slates, school books, maps, jewelry, silk reels, buttons, overalls, posters, children's books and even small furniture. You will search through these 1940's to 70's treasures with joy. They are true Proust madeleines!

11, rue Jean-Macé (11th).
M° Charonne, Faidherbe-Chaligny.
Phone: 01 43 72 02 83.

Au Grand Magasin

Les Petits Meubles de Marie

LES PETITS MEUBLES DE MARIE
PIMP MY FURNITURE

Marie Descamps is a specialist of small Parisian furniture. She bargain hunts dressers, tables and wardrobes. Then she restores and paints them in the Farrow & Ball tones. You can buy them at her studio-boutique. As a bonus: You can choose the color and other finishing touches before restoration.

38, rue Lucien-Sampaix (10th).
M° Jacques Bonsergent, Gare de l'Est.
Phone: 06 58 72 46 28.
lespetitsmeublesdemarie.fr

WHAT A LOVELY
BOUQUET!
FLORISTS UNLIKE ANY OTHERS

ARŌM PARIS
OLD-FASHIONED

In this store, generous and rustic bouquets favor ancient tones, and there is a beautiful selection of flowers in an antiquated atmosphere with mirrors and baroque chandeliers. Arrangements are created with good ideas, such as adding a branch of fresh mint for a perfumed finish. Home stylists love this place, which delivers in Paris and in the suburbs seven days a week.

73, avenue Ledru-Rollin (12th).
M° Ledru-Rollin.
Phone: 01 43 46 82 59.
aromparis.fr

Arôm Paris

Variations Végétales

VARIATIONS VÉGÉTALES
FRESH AIR

This florist sells only field-cultivated flowers from Ile-de-France. Greenhouse flowers and drip-fed tulips are not welcomed here! The plants have already lived through winter and are very resistant. Variations Végétales are experts at balcony and window plants and they make sure that the blooms in your window boxes will last. They even teach how to arrange and plant your own window boxes.

18, rue du Général-Guilhem (11th).
M° Rue St-Maur, Saint-Ambroise.
Phone: 01 43 55 22 45.
variationsvegetales.com

VÉRONIQUE PIEDELEU
DIRECTOR AT CARAVANE HOME DECOR STORES

HER FLORIST
FLOWER
"This has been the official florist of Caravane stores ever since it opened in Saint-Germain-des-Prés! This florist has wonderful flowers, poetic and creative in every season!"
14, rue des Saints-Pères (6th).
M° Saint-Germain-des-Prés, Rue du Bac.
Phone: 01 44 50 00 20. flower.fr

Les Mauvaises Graines

ATELIER VERTUMNE
HAPPY FIELDS
Field flowers are honored here. In this old studio, Clarisse Béraud and her team create poetic bouquets that look like tiny landscapes, and they vary depending on the shape of the vase. As a bonus, they organize a floral art course one week per month.
12, rue de la Sourdière (1st). M° Pyramides, Tuileries.
Phone: 01 42 86 06 76.
atelier-vertumne.fr

Atelier Vertumne

LES MAUVAISES GRAINES
ROCK AROUND THE FLOWERS
Nothing scares these "rock'n'roll gardeners": Sowing wild seeds or forgotten plants anywhere they please, this is their fun motto! It is the rule they go by to create balconies, smart gardens and landscape flowerbeds. A good way to get off the beaten track! Book an appointment at the showroom-shop in the 17th, or buy ready-made arrangements at the BHV.
5 bis, passage Geffroy-Didelot (17th). M° Villiers, Rome.
Phone: 01 40 67 13 40.
lesmauvaisesgraines.paris

La Fabrique Verte

LA FABRIQUE VERTE
FINE FLOWERS

Close to the Maison de la Radio, flowers bloom from floor to ceiling and onto the sidewalk; aromatic herbs grow in old wine cases; perennial plants live in beautiful concrete boxes. Florist Julie Commien offers numerous services: special designs for weddings, christenings or funerals, arrangements for balconies and terraces, as well as flower workshops for those who want to become horticulturist trainees.
35, rue Gros (16th).
RER Avenue du Président Kennedy, M° Jasmin.
Phone: 01 42 24 91 40.
lafabriqueverte.com

FIBRE VÉGÉTALE
GREAT ARRANGERS

The title of Meilleur Ouvrier de France (Best Worker in France) has been awarded to Muriel Le Couls. This florist from Mouffetard and her team welcome customers with a big smile and prepare a bundle of tulips with just as much care as a sumptuous bouquet. Seasonal flowers and plants invade the sidewalk.
Good quality, without the fuss.
51, rue Censier (5th). M° Censier-Daubenton.
Phone: 01 45 87 27 06.
fibre-vegetale.com

FLOWERS AT HOME, WITH OR WITHOUT A SUBSCRIPTION!

New floral designers have appeared on the Web. On the websites of Bergamotte and Flowerness, you can order classic-chic or rustic arrangements to be delivered within two hours or on a monthly subscription. At Bloom's, subscribe to receive seasonal flowers each month, along with greenery and ribbons to arrange a bouquet yourself. With Monsieur Marguerite, receive a rustic bouquet made in Sarthe each month, wherever you like.
Prices start at 29.90€ on bergamotte.com, 40€ on flowerness.fr, 30€ on monsieurmarguerite.com and 18€ on blooms.fr

Monsieur Marguerite

LES 2 AU COIN
FLOWERS AND FLAVORS

This little place combines a florist, beautiful cut flowers, flowerpot arrangements, caudex plants in different sizes (store specialty) and a restaurant, which is also a teahouse and co-working space. Delicious brunches are prepared here on Sundays. From morning to evening, breathe in the wonderful aromas of the food and fragrance of the flowers.

7, rue Notre-Dame-de-Bonne-Nouvelle (2nd).
M° Bonne Nouvelle, Strasbourg Saint-Denis.
Phone: 01 77 12 63 41.
les2aucoin.fr

L'ARROSOIR
ARTSY-CHIC

Decorated with chandeliers and bargain-hunted furniture — some for sale — L'Arrosoir is filled with magnificent flowers, tree and shrub branches, and small bouquets. Alain and Christine Bousquet work in an artsy atmosphere, give customers big smiles and arranging bouquets while listening to good music.

80, rue Oberkampf (11th). M° Parmentier.

DEBAULIEU
GRACEFUL

This is the latest favorite florist of all Parisian luxurious homes. Pierre Banchereau used to be a head-hunter but a new career as a florist means he now creates bouquets that mix strange or old-fashioned seasonal flowers with exotic greenery, ensuring a surprising and always elegant result.

30, rue Henry-Monnier (9th).
M° Pigalle, Saint-Georges. Phone: 01 45 26 78 68.
debaulieu-paris.com

Debaulieu

FOOD

PARIS IS A CITY FOR GOURMETS.
COME OVER HERE TO GROCERY SHOP!

FINE, VERY FINE
FOODS

PLACES WHERE THE BEST ARTISANS
SELL THE BEST PRODUCE

TERROIRS D'AVENIR
GOURMET ROAD

Alexandre and Samuel value produce
from local producers and supply the best
Parisian restaurants, as well as the stalls at
four locations. Fruit and vegetable producers,
butchers, fish dealers and bakers are stars in
this small street of Le Sentier — a fast-changing
neighborhood.

3-6-7-8, rue du Nil (2nd).

M° Sentier.

Phone: 01 85 09 84 00.

terroirs-avenir.fr

Terroirs d'Avenir

La Galerie Gourmande Balea

LA GALERIE
GOURMANDE BALEA
BEVERAGES AND SNACKS

This grocer focuses on three main produce:
wine, cheese and charcuterie. Jean-Luc
Sayegh knows how to find fruity Coteaux-du-
Languedoc or a beautiful Sauvignon de Loire
that is just as good as a Sancerre wine. Silvia
Balea does the same with the flowered tome,
truffle pecorino, morcilla and cecina from León,
for Iberian meat lovers. A wonderful pâté en
croûte and old-fashioned pies can be found
here too. We want more!

15, rue des Moines (17th). M° Brochant.

Phone: 01 42 63 31 40.

FOOD

PAPA SAPIENS
ORGANIC DELUXE

This is the fun name of a luxurious grocery store managed by six passionate small producer head-hunters. "Organic," "local" and "local food network": these are the principles they go by when selecting their produce. The pesto from Ella's garden is organic and super fresh, the lobster from Brittany is shelled and frozen, the duck is raised outdoors, and the fruit coulis from the Île-d'Yeu is organic... Take a tour of French traditional gastronomy.

32, rue de Bourgogne (7ᵗʰ). M° Varenne, Solférino.
Phone: 01 44 05 97 54.
7, rue Bayen (17ᵗʰ). M° Ternes.
Phone: 01 58 57 82 81.
papasapiens.fr

KILIKIO
THE TASTES OF GREECE

The best of Greece is here, organic and natural. At Kilikio you will find homemade olive oil, black pine tree or thyme honey, and many other fine produce. Gluten-free eaters will love the carob flour Cretan bread. The wine and alcohol selection (do not miss the mastika) comes from small vineyards and is not bad either. Everything comes straight from the producers, so the prices remain reasonable.

34, rue Notre-Dame-de-Nazareth (3ʳᵈ).
M° Temple, République.
Phone: 09 83 33 88 24.

Kilikio

THE GOOD IDEA

On the website of the Cretan village Adravasti, you can adopt an olive tree and help local producers. You will be guaranteed to receive organic and high-quality fair-trade olive oil. You can choose your tree by looking at photos, and pick a subscription depending on the number of liters of oil you want to receive in a year. You can also buy this as a gift for someone else.
adravasti.fr

PIERRE HERMÉ
PASTRY CHEF

HIS ITALIAN GROCER
LA TÊTE DANS LES OLIVES
"I love the olive oils that Cédric Casanova purchases from small producers in Sicily. He imports beautiful produce too, such as lemons, capers, oregano..."
2, rue Sainte-Marthe (10ᵗʰ).
M° Goncourt, Colonel Fabien.
Phone: 09 51 31 33 34.
latetedanslesolives.com

La Caravelle des Saveurs

LA CARAVELLE DES SAVEURS
PORTUGUESE DELICACIES

In this large and beautiful Portuguese grocer, you will find all typical produce from Portugal: canned sardines, Nata pastéis (egg custard tarts), cold meats and cheese. As a bonus: Lunch is provided on a large guest table, as well as snacking and evening beverages (menus start at 9.90€). Intense "saudade" here!

12, rue du Faubourg-Saint-Martin (10th).
M° Strasbourg Saint-Denis. Phone: 01 40 37 67 69.
lacaravelledessaveurs.paris

RACHEL'S GROCERY & DELI
JUST LIKE NEW YORK

Welcome to Rachel's grocery store, located on the other side of the road from the restaurant and teahouse (n°25) famous for its cheesecakes, pastries and other traditional American dishes. The three founders, Rachel and Birke Moeller and Maria Methodieva, designed this store, which is part grocery with produce mainly imported from the USA, and part deli, which carries homemade preparations such as beef pastrami, smoked fish, frankfurters, etc.

20, rue du Pont-aux-Choux (3rd).
M° Saint-Sébastien Froissart, Filles du Calvaire.

Umami Matcha Café

UMAMI MATCHA CAFĒ
MATCHA WANT?

Umami Matcha Café serves this Japanese green tea in hot or cold beverages, dishes and pastries. The distinctive feature here is the grocery store, managed by young French suppliers for great chefs. Find unpasteurized soy sauce, citrus ponzu, candied yuzu, black sesame paste – with advice and recipes to top it all off!

22, rue Béranger (3rd).
M° République.
Phone: 01 48 04 06 02.
umamiparis.com

Rachel's Grocery & Deli

FOOD

G. DETOU
2,400 SAFE BETS

G. Detou (it's a real name) is a landmark where house servants used to come for culinary goods even before the war. Instant or liquid egg whites, almonds and raisins of all kinds, pistachios and saffron from Iran, chocolate disks, licorice powder, rare mustard — 2,400 exceptional produce are sold here, packaged in large quantities to make pastry chefs and cooks happy. This is a favorite among future great chefs, who come here to find supplies for their culinary experiments.

58, rue Tiquetonne (2nd).
M° Étienne-Marcel.
Phone: 01 42 36 54 67.

LES ĒPICIERS MODERNES
THE BEST CHOICE

This is an Aladdin's cave of fine foods in Batignolles. You won't know what to choose in the amazing selection of wines and preserves, jars of dried produce, windows filled with butter and refined cheese by Jean-Yves Bordier, cold meats by Pedro Diego and Louis Ospital, and dishes prepared by La Table de Gascogne.

32, rue Boursault (17th).
M° Rome, Place de Clichy.
Phone: 09 51 67 92 54.

ANNE-SOPHIE PIC
STARRED CHEF

HER TEA SHOP
MAISON DE THĒ JUGETSUDO
"I am taken with the vast selection of teas offered by the 160 year-old Maison Jugetsudo. They work with great restaurants in Japan. I particularly love their green teas, such as the genmaïcha, the gyokuo and the sencha."

95, rue de Seine (6th).
M° Mabillon, Odéon.
Phone: 01 46 33 94 90.
jugetsudo.fr

Les Epiciers Modernes

CAUSSES
CHIC FOOD

This house offers general high-quality food supplies in three locations. They sell fruit, vegetables, meat, preserves, cakes, chocolate, pickles, dried fruit and unpackaged spices. You can also eat a small daily special there (for about 10€).

99, rue Rambuteau (1ˢᵗ). RER and M° Les Halles. Phone: 01 45 65 10 10.
222, rue Saint-Martin (3ʳᵈ). M° Étienne Marcel, Arts et Métiers. Phone: 01 42 71 33 33.
55, rue Notre-Dame-de-Lorette (9ᵗʰ). M° Saint-Georges, Pigalle. Phone: 01 53 16 10 10.
causses.org

Causses

L'ÉPICERIE VÉGÉTALE
GOOD AND ORGANIC

Half grocer and half florist, this is the place for organic lovers in the 11ᵗʰ. It is worth dropping by rue Fontaine-au-Roi. You will find rare and heirloom vegetables, specialties unseen elsewhere (such as black garlic from Japan), along with field flowers – and good advice to cook these reasonably priced produce.

51, rue de la Fontaine-au-Roi (11ᵗʰ). M° Goncourt, Parmentier. Phone: 06 73 35 62 11.

NEW LOCALES

The website Le Comptoir Local allows you to do your grocery shopping online at small producers' located within a 28-mile radius. Arrange your basket with a few clicks, and fill it with fruit, vegetables, dairy produce, meat, charcuterie, groceries. Everything is delivered within 48 hours, and without having to subscribe. How convenient!

lecomptoirlocal.fr

AU BOUT DU CHAMP
GOOD HARVEST
Fruit, vegetables and legumes!
In Batignolles, the store Au Bout du Champ displays cases filled with produce harvested every morning by local producers in Ile-de-France. Every day, from 8 a.m. to 10 p.m., you can come pick up your online order. You can also walk in and buy what you like.
20, rue des Dames (17th).
M° Place de Clichy, La Fourche.
118, rue Caulaincourt (18th).
M° Lamarck-Caulaincourt.
auboutduchamp.com

Meriggio

MERIGGIO
THE EXQUISITE HOUR
The Italian word "meriggio" refers to the sunniest hours of the day. Bastien and Laura Corinti are brother and sister, and their transalpine produce from the family farm offer sunshine to customers. Eat their Parma ham, which received several awards, the mountain Parmesan or mortadelle, with rare wines. Straight from Italy!
3, rue Rougemont (9th).
M° Grands Boulevards.
Phone: 07 78 82 45 74.

OBSESSIONAL
PASTRIES

BAKERS HIGHLY SPECIALIZED IN ĒCLAIRS, COOKIES, CHOUX BUNS...

Comme à Lisbonne

COMME Ā LISBONNE
BEST OF PORTUGAL

This is the Parisian place for Nata pastéis, a type of egg custard tart eaten lukewarm with or without cinnamon powder. Victor Silveira follows his mother's recipe. These delicacies come out of the oven twice a day in his two bakeries: the one in the Marais offers a Bairro Alto mood, whereas the most recent one in the Mogador area offers a chic counter and large shelves filled with groceries.

37, rue du Roi-de-Sicile (4th). M° Hôtel de Ville, Saint-Paul. Phone: 07 61 23 42 30 20.
20, rue de Mogador (9th). M° Chaussée d'Antin La Fayette, Trinité d'Estienne d'Orves. commealisbonne.com

MESDEMOISELLES MADELEINES
SOUVENIRS, SOUVENIRS

This bakery draws inspiration from luxury houses and offers haute-couture sweet and savory madeleines, and seasonal collections. Every day, four savory madeleines are prepared, along with fifteen sweet ones. Some are flavored, some filled or covered with a flavored shell, and all are available in different sizes and in cake form.

37, rue des Martyrs (9th).
M° Saint-Georges, Notre-Dame-de-Lorette.
Phone: 01 53 16 28 82. mllesmadeleines.com

Mesdemoiselles Madeleines

La Tarte Tropézienne

LA TARTE TROPÉZIENNE
CRÈME DE LA CRÈME

If you cannot go to Saint-Tropez, let this famous tart — the recipe of which is kept secret — come to you! These two bakeries in Paris sell the cream-filled sugary brioche in a medium, small or individual format. Soak up the sun all year long with this pastry, either in the classic version or with its limited edition seasonal flavours.

99, rue de Rivoli (1st).
M° Palais Royal-Musée du Louvre.
3, rue Montfaucon (6th). M° Mabillon.
Phone: 01 43 29 09 81.
latartetropezienne.fr

EAT PASTRIES WITHOUT PUTTING ON WEIGHT?

This is Eugène's promise, a baker who has started a war on sugar and fat. His breads, cakes, pastries, chocolates, ice creams and savory delicacies are for diabetics and gourmets who want to stay thin. Thanks, Eugène!

28, rue des Lombards (4th).
M° Châtelet.
Phone: 01 40 27 91 67.
11, rue Guillaume-Tell (17th).
M° Porte de Champerret.
Phone: 01 42 27 65 24.
eugene.paris

Eugène

O GÂTEAU
PAVLOVA PARADISE

This baker specializes in pavlova: a sublime mixture of Chantilly cream, meringue and fresh fruits. The meringue is light in sugar, crunchy and soft at the same time, and ornate with seasonal candied fruit and white chocolate ganache. Brioches and lava cakes are also offered.

135, rue des Pyrénées (20th).
M° Alexandre Dumas, Maraîchers.
Phone: 01 43 67 70 23.

O Gâteau

FOU DE PÂTISSERIE
DREAM TEAM

The team of the eponymous magazine launched this store, which provides a selection of cakes baked by famous Parisian pastry chefs all in one location. You will not have to run around to eat a rose Ispahan by Hermé, an Equinoxe by Lignac, or a Phil'Goût by Conticini — they are all here, delivered each morning in individual portions. Gilles Marchal's candy is also available.

45, rue Montorgueil (2nd).
M° Les Halles, Étienne Marcel.
Phone: 01 40 41 00 61.

Scoop Me a Cookie

Fou de Pâtisserie

SCOOP ME A COOKIE
CRISPY AND CRUNCHY

In this cookie shop, generosity is key.
The cookies are soft with crunchy edges, and the ingredients are chosen carefully: AOC butter from Charentes, organic eggs, Piedmont nuts, Grand Cru Valrhona® chocolate. The cookies are available in different formats, and we particularly love the "giant" ones, which should be shared and eaten like a cake.

5-7, rue Crespin-du-Gast (11th). M° Ménilmontant.
Phone: 01 73 74 28 90.
72, rue Legendre (17th).
M° La Fourche, Rome.
Phone: 01 71 72 91 65.
scoopmeacookie.com

Odette

L'Atelier de l'Éclair

L'ATELIER DE L'ÉCLAIR
INCREDIBLY GOOD

This boutique is actually a culinary laboratory, which revisits the éclair, sweet and savory, with a light choux pastry and refined flavors. The result is a large counter that features twelve "classic sweet" éclairs, and six "savory clubs" a day, made in front of you and in XL format. Choose from lemon and meringue, salted caramel, milk foam and hazelnut, dry ham with tomato and mozzarella, smoked salmon and cucumber – L'Atelier de l'Éclair offers a catering service and "cocktail" creations to die for.

9, rue Bachaumont (2nd). M° Sentier.
Phone: 01 82 09 34 21. latelierdeleclair.fr

ODETTE
SO PUFFY

Chez Odette, come enjoy cream-filled puffs made of choux pastry, which come in nine different flavors: chocolate, caramel, berries, green tea, praline, etc. These delicious pastries are presented in chic boxes decorated with a monogram, and you can order a wedding cake. We strongly recommend the store in the 5th. The historic building has a terrace and teahouse with a view from the first floor on Notre-Dame de Paris.

18, rue Montorgueil (1st). RER and M° Les Halles.
Phone: 01 40 41 03 79.
77, rue Galande (5th). RER and M° Saint-Michel, Cluny-La Sorbonne. Phone: 01 43 26 13 06.
odette-paris.com

MARIE-HÉLÈNE DE TAILLAC
JEWELRY DESIGNER

HER PATISSERIE
LA MAISON DU CHOU
"I am a fan of this place, which makes sublime cream puffs. My favorite flavor is the classic with cream cheese!"
7, rue de Fürstenberg (6th).
M° Mabillon, Saint-Germain-des-Prés.
Phone: 09 54 75 06 05.

IME

.E FINGER
NG YOUR TEA!

L'Oisive Thé

L'OISIVE THÉ
KNITTING AREA

This is a teahouse and a small needlecraft department, all in one. You can enjoy tea and a pastry, then choose yarn (among several brands, including the house brand, La Bien Aimée) and a model to knit a snood, a sweatshirt or a scarf. Your knitting neighbors will share tips with you. You'll never be bored at L'Oisive Thé!

8 bis, rue de la Butte-aux-Cailles (13ᵗʰ).
M° Place d'Italie. Phone: 01 53 80 31 33.
loisivethe.com

Sébastien Gaudard

SÉBASTIEN GAUDARD
SO CHARMING

After the rue des Martyrs, Sébastien Gaudard is electrifying the Tuileries. On the first floor: pastries. On the second floor: a charming teahouse where you can escape the Paris rush for a sweet or savory ceremony. Eggs Florentine, croque-monsieur (known to be the best in Paris) and traditional pastries (light in sugar and fat), including house specials such as the Mussipontain and the Duchesse (the ancestor of the éclair), are all on the menu.

1, rue des Pyramides (1ˢᵗ).
M° Tuileries, Pyramides.
Phone: 01 71 18 24 70.

MAMIE GĀTEAUX
RETRO SO GOOD

In the heart of the 6th, the well-named Mamie Gâteaux (meaning "Grandma's cakes") treats customers to lunches and snacks composed of delicious soups, savory tarts, salads with salmon or ham, and dozens of pastries that change each day (cherry-pistachio or almond-fig tarts). Enjoy this in a retro environment, with a collection of old bowls on the shelves, plates on the walls and grandma's lace drapes.

66, rue du Cherche-Midi (6th).
M° Saint-Placide, Vaneau.
Phone: 01 42 22 32 15.

CHAMBELLAND
GLUTEN FREE

Everything is home-made in this gluten-free teahouse bakery, starting with the flour, which comes from Chambelland mill. On the menu, special breads are sides to salads, and focaccia sandwiches are filled with tuna, organic salmon or pickled haddock.
On the sweet side, try the chocolate lava cake or the fruit tarts (the lemon tart is so yummy!), which are popular among regulars, including those not allergic to gluten.

14, rue Ternaux (11th). M° Oberkampf.
Phone: 01 43 55 07 30.
chambelland.com

MYRIAM DE LOOR
CO-FOUNDER OF PETIT PAN

HER TEAHOUSE
LILY OF THE VALLEY

"This is a 'small garden with wonderful smells of the metropolitan' in the middle of Paris. In this teahouse reigns a subtle mixture of nostalgia, romanticism and modernity. I love the plants that grow on the ceiling and on the wallpaper. And, most of all, I love the smell of tea that spreads in the air."

12, rue Dupetit-Thouars (3rd).
M° Temple. Phone: 01 57 40 82 80.

GOOD
COFFEE

INTIMATE COFFEE SHOPS TO FORGET BIG COFFEE CHAINS

TEN BELLES
GOURMET

Ten Belles was created by a French and English couple of baristas, already known for managing the excellent Bal Café in the 18th. The coffee comes from the Brûlerie de Belleville; the homemade cakes have built a strong reputation for this place (such as the Guinness-peanut butter chocolate or the raspberry-frangipane tart), and the British-inspired salads and sandwiches are a delight.

10, rue de la Grange-aux-Belles (10th).
M° Jacques Bonsergent. Phone: 01 42 40 90 78.
17, rue Breguet (11th). M° Bastille.

Ten Belles

La Caféothèque

LA CAFÉOTHÈQUE
ETHICAL

Gloria Montenegro, an ex-ambassador for Guatemala, opened this Caféothèque to highlight fair-trade grand cru coffees, most of them organic. This unique place is a coffee shop and a school for people who want to open coffee shops. The freshly ground coffee can also be taken to go, along with gluten-free cakes by L'Atelier des Lilas.

52, rue de l'Hôtel-de-Ville (4th).
M° Pont Marie.
Phone: 01 53 01 83 84.
lacafeotheque.com

FOOD

CAFÉ COUTUME
LUMINOUS

A counter with white tiles, a glass roof, this New-York style coffee shop and restaurant does everything right! The coffee machine roasts grand cru grains on the spot for Café Coutume and other coffee shops in the city. The ground coffee can be bought to go, along with machines to make your own coffee at home. A bonus: Delicious homemade pastries.

47, rue de Babylone (7th).
M° Saint-François-Xavier.
Phone: 01 45 51 50 47.
coutumecafe.com

KB Cafeshop

KB CAFESHOP
THE TRAVELER

A cool Anglophone vibe reigns in this coffee shop, opened by a Frenchman in love with Australia. Espressos are made by baristas who learned their job in New Zealand. Cappucino, latte, ristretto, the menu is about fifteen flavors long, and you can enjoy your drink on blond wooden tables or on the terrace of avenue Trudaine. Tarts, cakes, salads, sandwiches and homemade fruit juices are also available at all times.

53, avenue Trudaine (9th). M° Pigalle.
Phone: 09 66 13 79 10.

VALÉRIE GERBI
FASHION DIRECTOR
AT MERCI

HER COFFEE SHOP
HOLYBELLY
"I love this new trend: Coffee shops where you can drink delicious coffee with milk foam and eat a real brunch on weekends."
19, rue Lucien-Sampaix (10th).
M° Jacques-Bonsergent.
holybel.ly

CRAFT
THE HARD WORKER

This coworking space is a step away from République and looks something like a coffee shop, especially because you can taste excellent, freshly ground coffee here, along with pastries and homemade savory tarts. Twenty-two working spaces are available, several of which are located around a large table, as well as a special lounging space for meetings. It costs 3€ an hour, deducted from the cost of your drinks.

24, rue des Vinaigriers (10th). M° Jacques Bonsergent.
Phone: 01 40 35 90 77.
cafe-craft.com

ICE PALACES

CREAM OR SORBET, RICH OR LIGHT – HERE'S WHERE YOU CAN TREAT YOURSELF

UNE GLACE Ā PARIS
HOMEMADE SURPRISES

This is the gourmet place.
Artisans work in the basement to smoke chocolate disks with beech wood, among other things. Meanwhile, customers have the hard task of choosing among gourmet ice creams, sorbets flavored with surprising fruit, frozen pastries, milk shakes and iced beverages made on the spot from fresh fruit and a scoop of sorbet.
15, rue Sainte-Croix-de-la-Bretonnerie (4th).
M° Hôtel de Ville.
Phone: 01 49 96 98 33.
une-glace-a-paris.fr

GLAZED
ICED CREATIONS

In the ice world, Glazed ice creams stand out with unusual creations, such as the retrogressive Popcorn flavor, made from pop-corn and caramel with a little pepper, or the inebriating Tokyo Mojito, a sorbet made with rum, fresh mint and organic lemon. We also love the milk shakes, iced desserts (tarts, vacherins, cheesecake and Yule log), and the revisited Belgian waffles.
54, rue des Martyrs (9th).
M° Pigalle, Saint-Georges.
Phone: 09 81 62 47 06.
glaces-glazed.com

A TASTE OF SAINT-TROPEZ

In the chic DS Café locations, treat yourself to homemade ice cream by the Saint-Tropez brand Barbarac. It is made from natural produce and follows pure Italian tradition.
They even offer eight ultra light (sugar-free) flavors: natural, raspberry, blueberry, lemon, peach, vanilla, chocolate and coffee. Enjoy, guilt-free!
3, rue de Sontay (16th). M° Victor Hugo.
Phone: 01 45 01 21 21.
25, avenue Niel (17th). M° Ternes.
Phone: 01 40 55 02 02.
Delivery service: 01 42 27 28 50.
dscafe.fr

FOOD

IL GELATO DEL MARCHESE
ORIGINAL TREATS

This retro-chic place honors the recipes of the Italian ice cream maker Marco Radicioni. Surprising savory flavors, such as the Parmesan and pine nut ice cream, can be found next to traditional fruit sorbets and prestigious creations (pistachio and honey Croccante Fiorentino, hazelnut, almond and sesame). The classical music playing and white and gold decorations turn this into an enchanted parenthesis within the city.

3, rue des Quatre-Vents (6th). M° Odéon.
Phone: 01 46 34 75 63.

Une Glace à Paris

Il Gelato del Marchese

DIP & GO
WANDERING CONES

These homemade ice creams prepared from natural and fresh ingredients come in thirty-five flavors, to be discovered at the Saint-Germain parlor or on the traveling, bicycle-operated carts and Piaggio truck. Even better, the house special – the Frozen Yogurt – is guaranteed 0% fat, until you start adding delicious toppings!

5, rue de Montfaucon (6th).
M° Mabillon.
Phone: 09 84 28 47 55.
dip-and-go.com

ICEROLL
WELL ROLLED

This Parisian ice cream maker had a wonderful idea. In front of his clients, he makes ice cream rolls from all-natural produce! The iceRoller places a thin layer of liquid natural ice cream and the selected flavor (fresh fruit mash, salted caramel, etc.) on a cold plate. A few seconds later, he forms rolls and adds toppings upon request.

7, rue de Turenne (4th).
M° Saint-Paul.
iceroll.fr

iceRoll

RESTAURANTS

SAVOIR VIVRE ALSO MEANS
KNOWING HOW, AND WHERE, TO EAT.
BON APPĒTIT!

DELICIOUS
CAFÉS

SMALL RESTAURANTS THAT SERVE MOUTHWATERING FOOD

PUCE
WORLD GASTRONOMY

This tiny place is open from noon to midnight and run by a woman from Singapore and a wine lover. It offers a list of refined wines adapted to the small food portions, designed to be shared. On the menu: Guacamole made on the spot, grilled razor clams, pork croquettes, shells, lemongrass and ginger, macaroni and cheese (from 3 to 13€). The menu offers a wide range of food that will delight your taste buds.

1, rue Chaptal (9th). M° Pigalle, Saint-Georges.
Phone: 09 53 48 29 75.
ilovepuce.com

Puce

116 Pages

116 PAGES
FRENCH-JAPANESE

Although the little brother of the gourmet restaurant Pages, and located just a few steps away, this is a bristro with an unpolished decor. You can taste French-Japanese fusion food cooked on sumibiyaki – a type of barbecue. You can order one of a hundred natural wines by the glass, along with craft beers from all over and revisited cocktail classics. Beverages start at 5€, and the dishes range from 3€ to 40€.

2, rue Auguste-Vacquerie (16th).
M° Kléber, George V. Phone: 01 47 20 10 45.

LE BICHAT
SLOW DELIGHTS

This café honors slow, 100-percent organic and homemade food. Every day, the team creates recipes with pork, chicken, egg or mackerel that will accompany a bowl of rice, vegetables or crudités. Prices are between 8 and 9€. Dishes are taken to go, or can be eaten on the terrace, on high chairs in the main room or sitting comfortably in the mezzanine.

11, rue Bichat (10th).

M° Goncourt, République.

Phone: 09 54 27 68 97.

lebichat.fr

Le Bichat

LA RECYCLERIE
GREEN POWER

Set in an old train station, this restaurant functions by the three R's: reduce, reuse and recycle. As a result, the café offers dishes with less meat as well as vegetable-based recipes. The kitchen scraps are given to the animals of the urban farm for food. From 8€ to 12.50€ for a dish.

83, boulevard Ornano (18th). M° Porte de Clignancourt.

Phone: 01 42 57 58 49.

larecyclerie.com

GIGI
BEST CREPES

This place was created by the same team as the restaurant Aller Retour (3rd), and is the ideal creperie for a girl's night out. They even offer a snack menu "bites," which lets you taste a little of everything. Our favorite crepes: Duck breast with pear and blue cheese, and organic shrimp with avocado and mango. For heavy eaters, organic buckwheat pancakes are also on the menu. Menu: 12€ for six bites.

4, rue de la Corderie (3rd).

M° Temple, Filles du Calvaire. Phone: 07 83 58 75 30.

DELIVERED

Deliveroo and Foodora are two apps that feature menus from restaurants within a 2-mile radius. You can choose your food, pay online (add an extra 2.50€ for delivery) and monitor the preparation of your food, as well as the delivery status directly on your smartphone. Delivery within 30 minutes.

deliveroo.fr, foodora.fr

Apps available for free on the App Store and Google Play.

Claudette

CLAUDETTE
IN REAL TIME

A beautiful location decorated with hanging plants. It is open from breakfast to dinner, and has a terrace for when it gets warm – we feel good at Claudette's. On the menu: Small tapas-sized cooked dishes, salmon tatakis, ginger-candied sweet potatoes, high-end charcuterie, natural wines and local hard cider. For dessert, try the guava and raspberry panna cotta. You can also eat at the counter in front of the chef, in the basement. What could be better? 16€ for 2 dishes.

47, rue de Turbigo (3rd).
M° Arts et Métiers.
Phone: 01 40 24 10 36.

BUVETTE
FROM MORNING TO EVENING

The well-named Gastrothèque is the Parisian variation of Jodie's New York restaurant. With her associate Thomas, she serves cooked meals made from local, organic and seasonal produce, starting at breakfast. In the evening, the menu offers small plates of vegetables (from 7€), fish (from 9€) or meat (from 10€). Take note: This restaurant does not take reservations.

28, rue Henry-Monnier (9th). M° Pigalle.
Phone: 01 44 63 41 71.
paris.ilovebuvette.com

RESTAURANTS

MG ROAD AND DESI ROAD
INDIAN SONG

Stéphanie de Saint Simon offers the very best from India. She offers home decor items with her brand Ouma Productions, and two Bombay-inspired bistros. In the first bistro, beautiful produce and street food classics mix, including the must-eat scallop soufflés. In the second bistro, individual dishes served on a metal platter, Thalis, are ideal for tasting a large selection of typical dishes.

MG Road : 205, rue Saint-Martin (3rd).
M° Étienne Marcel, Rambuteau. Phone: 01 42 76 04 32.
mgroadrestaurant.com

Desi Road : 14, rue Dauphine (6th).
M° Saint-Michel, Odéon. Phone: 01 43 26 44 91.
desiroadrestaurant.com

Blueberry Maki Bar

THE FRIENDLY APP

"Do you want to know about a restaurant in the neighborhood?" There's no need to ask your friends – Bim gathers your friends', and friends of friends' impressions on restaurants from all over the world. The places are rated and commented by people close to you, and with a simple click, you can check availabilities and book a table.

Free on the App Store and Google Play

BLUEBERRY MAKI BAR
SUSHI FROM THE FUTURE

In this sushi bar, you can order California makis, sushis (of course!) and fusion makis. The decor is kawaii with paper lanterns and bright colors on the walls, and you will taste wonderful and flavorful Japan-inspired tapas. Truffle, raspberry, smoked mozzarella, Espelette pepper, all ingredients trigger the chef Luu's unlimited imagination. Between 35€ and 50€ on the menu.

6, rue du Sabot (6th). M° Saint-Sulpice, Saint-Germain-des-prés. Phone: 01 42 22 21 56.

LE VERRE VOLĒ SUR MER
TOP BENTOS

This is the second location for the Verre Volé team. Be careful: This place can accomodate only eighteen people, so make a reservation! For lunch, Maori Murota cooks surprising bentos. For dinner, Olive Davoux creates small sea platters with Asian or Italian influences, depending on the day. As for beverages, the natural wines are a good find! Lunch bentos at 14€. Dinner menu at 32€.

53, rue de Lancry (10th). M° Jacques Bonsergent. Phone: 01 48 03 21 38.

HEALTHY FOOD

EATING DELICIOUS AND LIGHT FOOD IS POSSIBLE!

RICE TROTTERS
SO RICE!

This café surfs on the single-produce trend by creating recipes with rice, in its 70,000 varieties. Starred chef Anthony Boucher cooks here, and at l'Apibo (31, rue Tiquetonne, 2nd). The menu offers rice portions in many different shapes and flavors: risotto, dishes with a red, pink or black rice base, a "patisse rice," rice pudding, perfect for those who eat gluten-free. The menu starts at 11.90€.

22, rue du Colisée (8th).
M° Saint-Philippe-du-Roule.
Phone: 01 53 75 11 95.
ricetrotters.com

Rice Trotters

LA VERRIÈRE
MIND AND BODY

This place combines an art gallery, a spa (with osteopathy, hydromassages and iyashi dome) and a vegetarian restaurant. Lunch is served as a buffet each day, made up of salads, soups and desserts. The decor is completely white, and you can fill your plate with sautéed vegetables, red lentils with Swiss chard, stuffed eggplant, etc. Do not miss the squash and carrot soup, the celery fries and the vegan ragout. Prices turn around 15€.

24, avenue de Tourville (7th).
M° École Militaire.
Phone: 01 77 18 39 16.

LES PETITES CASSEROLES

Don't bother thinking about cooking when you get home from work. On Sunday for a Tuesday delivery, or on Wednesday for Friday, you can plan your dinners online on Petites Casseroles' website. If you can't plan that far ahead, the "express" mode lets you order a delivery for that very day – albeit with a reduced selection. Everything is homemade and seasonal, and vacuum-packed for longer preservation. Enjoy a meal for 8.50€. Prices are on a sliding scale if you order several meals.

lespetitescasseroles.fr

RESTAURANTS

WILD & THE MOON
VENI VEDI VEGGIE

In this café/salad bar/juice bar, everything is organic, vegetarian, sometimes vegan, homemade and delicious. The setting is warm and welcoming without overdoing it: white walls decorated with a plant forest and a glass roof. Try the brown rice, kale, black radish, carrots, and avocado cream salad with kale chips. You can eat there or take your food to go. Free choice on the menu for about 20€.
55, rue Charlot (3rd).
M° Filles du Calvaire.
Phone: 09 51 80 22 33.
wildandthemoon.com

Wild & The Moon

IM THAÏ GOURMET
FRIEND OF THE LADIES

This gourmet restaurant is perfect for an all-girl lunch. It is a good idea to order one of the three full menus (appetizer, main course, dessert), A, B or C, which offer reasonable portions. Try the papaya salad, beef curry and a small portion of the Thai dessert. It is delicious, savory and sates your appetite — perfect to avoid snacking in the afternoon. Tables are set well apart so you and your friends can really talk. Menu starts at 18€.
8, rue Port-Mahon (2rd).
M° Quatre-Septembre, Opéra.
Phone: 01 47 42 63 82.
imrestaurant.fr

Nous

NOUS
ALL TASTES

Nous is held by Henri Kerveillant, who is gluten-intolerant, and Paula Piétri, who is in the process of becoming a vegetarian. This young couple has opened two canteens, where everyone (whether a vegetarian, meat-eater, organic-addict or gluten-intolerant) can find the right dish, between the Nourger, the Nous bowl, the Noupe or the Nourrito, available in different flavors. From 12€ to 14€ for a formula.

8, rue de Châteaudun (9th). M° Cadet, Notre-Dame-de-Lorette. Phone: 09 50 51 58 82.

16, rue de Paradis (10th). M° Gare de l'Est, Château d'Eau. Phone: 09 80 92 72 10.

nousrestaurant.fr

L'OPÉRA RESTAURANT
LYRICAL FOOD

The restaurant at the Opera house offers light food for dancers, and gastronomical dishes for its chic nocturnal clientele. Chihiro Yamazaki trained with Ducasse and delights her customers with healthy food. The classified architecture mixes with a pop decor. To fight calories, choose the vegetable stew with lotus roots, daikon, bok choy cabbage, shimeji and broth. It is perfect to stay fit, and very good for your health. The menu is 37€.

Palais Garnier. 1, place Jacques-Rouché (9th). M° Opéra, Chaussée d'Antin La Fayette. Phone: 01 42 68 86 80. opera-restaurant.fr

L'Opéra Restaurant

CANTINE VAGABONDE
ALL-ORGANIC

In this working-class neighborhood
that has yet to be gentrified, the Cantine
Vagabonde offers refined eaters a gourmet
vegetarian cuisine. For lunch, dinner or on the
weekends, Lila Djeddi roasts sweet potatoes
with a citrus sauce; fennel, red onion and blue
cheese tarts or apple-pear crisps. Everything is
organic and inexpensive, and served in a
lovely bargain-hunted decor. Lunch formulas
start at 14.50€. Dinner is fixed at 25€.

11, rue d'Aubervilliers (18th).
M° Stalingrad.
Phone: 01 46 07 44 89.
cantinevagabonde.fr

NANASHI
THE BENTO SHOW

In this hipster café, people come to eat the
organic bento of the day and the fresh fruit
juices. The decor is stripped down with light
wooden chairs, a blackboard and paper
lanterns. This is the right place for a lunch or a
family brunch. Ā la carte for about 25€.

57, rue Charlot (3rd).M° Filles du Calvaire.
Phone: 09 60 00 25 59.
31, rue de Paradis (10th).
M° Poissonnière.
Phone: 01 40 22 05 55.
nanashi.fr

Cantine Vagabonde

TASTY HOMEMADE DISHES

Frichtie defines itself as a "happiness delivery service," with reasonably priced little dishes
made by a team trained alongside starred chefs. Choose your meal among about twenty
suggestions on the website. It will be delivered on an electric scooter within 30 minutes, at noon
and for dinner, every day of the week. Appetizers from 2.20€, main courses from 5.90€ and
desserts from 1.80€. Add 1.50€ for normal delivery, or 2,40€ for express delivery.
Phone: 01 76 35 01 74. frichti.co

Café Pinson

CAFÉ PINSON
ENERGIZING

These are two great locations to re-charge your batteries! Café Pinson offers 100-percent organic fruit and vegetables, fresh juices and smoothies, vegetarian daily specials with plenty of grains, a vegan menu made from gluten-free flour and cereals.

6, rue du Forez (3rd). M° Filles du Calvaire.
Phone: 09 83 82 53 53.
58, rue du Faubourg-Poissonnière (10th).
M° Cadet, Poissonnière.
Phone: 01 45 23 59 42.
cafepinson.fr

LA PETITE FABRIQUE
THRILLING

This organic restaurant is appealing
with large windows and light wooden furniture. The menu is just as thrilling, with a choice of gourmet dishes, such as cod brandade, vegetable tajine, squash and comté cheese tart, with a side of roasted vegetables. You can end your meal with a dessert that will remind you of your childhood: pecan pie or chocolate lava cake? About 30€.

15, rue des Vignoles (20th). M° Buzenval, Avron.
Phone: 01 43 73 57 88.

LE POUTCH
GUARANTEED GLUTEN-FREE

This is a girly place with a fresh decor,
perfect to eat vegetarian and gluten-free dishes or take them to go: salads, sandwiches, quiches and soups. Seasonal produce is used, the portions are small, which is great if you want to try different dishes, and the menu changes every week. Good to know:
There are a few tables outside to eat in the sun. The lunch set menu is 11€. No reservations.

13, rue Lucien-Sampaix (10th). M° Jacques Bonsergent.
Phone: 09 53 70 90 83. lepoutch.fr

My Free Kitchen

MY FREE KITCHEN
100-PERCENT ORGANIC

This is a gluten-free, lactose-free and 100-percent organic café and grocery shop. Lunch set menus offer a choice between the salad, soup, savory cake, quiche and daily special. Dinner is served hot: bruschetta, pizza or cooked meal with a mezze. This gourmet and healthy spot also serves brunch on Saturdays. Set menus start at 10.90€ for lunch, and 13€ for dinner.

1 bis, rue Bleue (9th). M° Cadet, Poissonnière.
Phone: 01 48 01 67 64.
myfreekitchen.com

MAJESTIC AT THE (JUICE) BAR!

New Yorker Marc Grossman started the trend in Paris with Bob's Juice Bar and two other locations, where he serves his vitamin-filled juices. Nubio appeared later, providing cold-pressed, non-pasteurized organic juices. Detox Delight started the home detox trend. Recently, the model Mareva Galanter and nutritionist Valérie Espinasse attracted a lot of attention for opening Good Organic Only. Four locations to detox with juices!

Bob's Juice Bar :
15, rue Lucien-Sampaix (10th).
M° Jacques Bonsergent.
Phone: 09 50 06 36 18.
bobsjuicebar.com

Bob's Kitchen :
74, rue des Gravilliers (3rd).
M° Arts et Métiers.
Phone: 09 52 55 11 66.

Bob's Bake Shop :
Halle Pajol, 12, esplanade Nathalie-Sarraute (18th).
M° Marx Dormoy.
Phone: 09 84 46 25 26.

L'Atelier Nubio :
4, rue Paul-Bert (11th).
M° Rue des Boulets, Faidherbe-Chaligny.
Phone: 09 84 35 51 13.
nubio.fr

Detox Delight : 106, rue Amelot (11th).
M° Filles du Calvaire.
Phone: 01 80 96 31 70.
detox-delight.fr

Good Organic Only :
17, rue des Archives (4th).
M° Hôtel de Ville.
Phone: 01 40 71 10 03
and 41, avenue Kléber (16th). M° Boissière.
goodorganiconly.com

BRUNCH,
ALWAYS

ON WEEKENDS, WITH FAMILY OR FRIENDS, BRUNCH IS ALWAYS A SAFE BET

PANCAKE SISTERS
WEEKDAY BRUNCH

Pancake Sisters delights us with sweet and savory pancakes that come in all flavors. The house special is the panster (a sandwich made from two pancakes), and this place distinguishes itself by offering weekday brunches. The brunch is bigger on weekends: it has a larger choice of main courses, as well as sweet and savory add-ons. Weekdays at 19.50€, 23.50€ on weekends.

3, rue Lucien-Sampaix (10th). M° Jacques Bonsergent.
Phone: 09 83 33 30 23.
pancakesisters.com

Pancake Sisters

Sésame

SÉSAME
A TERRACE WITH A VIEW

Great smells, great flavors and a relaxed atmosphere – this is Sésame. You can go there to enjoy the terrace with a view on the canal Saint-Martin and its carefully chosen local produce. The entire neighborhood meets there on weekends to eat a classic brunch with hot beverages, homemade jam, organic eggs, bagels and fresh smoothies. 24€ for brunch.

51, quai de Valmy (10th). M° République.
Phone: 01 42 49 03 21.
au-sesame.com

RESTAURANTS

LES CROCS DES HALLES
FOR AN OGRE'S APPETITE

Vegetarians, beware! This place is reminiscent of the Halles traditional meat markets. The meat is cured on the spot and ordered by the kilogram. Brunch features an assortment of meat (small portions of sausage, tartare, and steak) with a side of fries. The menu is completed with fresh fruit and pastries for huge appetites!
38€ for a butcher's brunch.
49, rue Berger (1ᵉʳ).
M° Louvre-Rivoli, Les Halles.
Phone: 01 40 28 00 00.

LES 400 COUPS
@ LA CINÉMATHÈQUE
CHILD-FRIENDLY

For families and singles, this is the go-to place on weekends. Les 400 Coups is inside the Cinémathèque française, located near the entrance of the Bercy park. Another reason you should go there is that the brunch serves organic and local produce, and toys are offered to children when the weather does not permit outdoor fun. Brunch is 23€.
51, rue de Bercy (12ᵗʰ).
M° Bercy.
Phone: 01 43 44 18 72.
les400coupsalacinematheque.fr

Alphonse et Madeleine

Les 400 Coups @ la Cinémathèque

BREAKFAST AT HOME

· On Alphonse and Madeleine's website or on the phone, choose an organic breakfast set menu by 4 p.m. for the next morning. Delivery starts at 8:30 a.m., with flowers (add 10€) or the morning paper (newsstand price). Starts at 14.50€ per person Phone: 06 62 88 43 99.
alphonseetmadeleine.com

· Good Morning's website was made for businesses, but private individuals can also place orders. Breakfast orders have to be placed 48 hours in advance; they are for two and include pastries from Pâtisserie des Rêves, granola by Catherine Kluger and Kusmi Teas to start off the day! 55€.
goodmorning-paris.com

La Maison Bleue

LA MAISON BLEUE
MARKET CUISINE

This blue house is not on a hill, but it opens onto a delightful square. However, the charm of this place is not only due to its view and terrace. At the table, the market cuisine is a delight. On Sundays, the brunch is super fresh, made up of freshly pressed fruit juices, organic granola, salted-caramel French toast, Iberian ham, truffle scrambled eggs. We would gladly spend all day there! Brunch is 25€.

7, place Franz-Liszt (10th). M° Poissonnière.
Phone: 01 44 65 01 80.
lamaisonbleue.paris

LES GRANDS VOISINS
FAIR-TRADE ATMOSPHERE

The former hospital Saint-Vincent-de-Paul became the headquarters of charities that accomodate residents, workshops and a small restaurant. It is open to the public on weekends and offers a cool vibe reminiscent of Berlin. The brunch is made up of a platter, a green salad, a dessert and a hot beverage (13€). To top it all off, it has a terrace with a garden and organizes workshops for children.

82, avenue Denfert-Rochereau (14th).
M° Denfert-Rochereau, RER Port-Royal.
Phone: 07 83 76 21 00.
lesgrandsvoisins.org

LIZA
ALL-YOU-CAN-EAT MEZZE

This is the best Lebanese restaurant in Paris, and the most elegant with its refined decor, which features young designers from Beirut. It serves brunch on weekends. The buffet provides all-you-can-eat mezze (hummus, bean and peas ragout, tabbouleh, bites), hot seasonal dishes, as well as orange blossom flan, pastries and fruit salad for dessert — all of this for 34€, absolutely justified!

14, rue de la Banque (2nd). M° Bourse.
Phone: 01 55 35 00 66.
restaurant-liza.com

L'ENTREPÔT
CULTURE & FOOD

This movie theater and its restaurant have well earned their great reputation. In this multicultural spot, you can watch movies, listen to concerts and see shows. The restaurant offers Sunday brunch with a gigantic buffet of hot and cold seasonal plates, charcuterie, cheese, smoked fish, along with sweet and savory tarts. Enjoy your meal on the patio or in the quiet garden. Brunch is 31€.

7, rue Francis-de-Pressensé (14th).
M° Pernety.
Phone: 01 45 40 07 50.
lentrepot.fr

IKRA
AS IN RUSSIA

Ikra, not Ikea! This is a great place to enjoy Russian tapas. In the original tongue, they are called "zakouskis." On weekends, Ikra serves a gourmet brunch: pepper caviar, smoked salmon, pirogi (small stuffed pasta), borsch (cabbage and beet soup), tarts or cottage cheese... Brunch is 26€.

119, boulevard Raspail (6th).
M° Notre-Dame-des-Champs.
Phone: 01 45 48 12 33.
ikra-paris.com

À LA FOLIE
CHILDREN'S PARTY

This festive place hosts families on weekends. Brunch is made up of barbecued fish, chicken or pork chops and salads — for consuming at large tables or on deckchairs on the grass of the Villette park. Games for children. Brunch set menu is 45€, and a dish is 14€.

26, avenue Corentin-Cariou (19th).
M° Porte de la Villette.
Phone: 07 76 79 70 66.

**MORGANE
SEZALORY**
FASHION DESIGNER
FOR SÉZANE

HER PASTRY SHOP
LA LIBERTÉ

"I love Benoît Castel's bread and cakes, especially his cream tart. I often eat brunch on Sunday in his pastry shop in Ménilmontant. La Liberté (Freedom), what a beautiful name!"

150, rue de Ménilmontant (20th). M° Pelleport, Saint-Fargeau. Phone: 01 46 36 13 82.
39, rue des Vinaigriers. M° Jacques Bonsergent (10th). Phone: 01 42 05 51 76.
libertepatisserieboulangerie.com

À la Folie

THE A **GAME**

PARTICULARLY DELICIOUS GOURMET RESTAURANTS

HERO
KOREAN HARMONY

This Korean restaurant has got it all: great service, a fun and vibrant decor, and a cuisine that will leave you with nothing but good memories. The Canadian chef spent time in Korea and developed a fusion cuisine. Our favorite dish is the yangnyeom fried chicken, with a plain or spicy crust. Other delicious plates: the pork chop buns, the jellyfish and green apple salad and the shiitake cooked rice cakes. This place also has a cocktail bar with surprising mixtures. 35€ à la carte.

289, rue Saint-Denis (2nd). M° Strasbourg Saint-Denis.
heroparis.com

Hero

La Marée Jeanne

LA MARĒE JEANNE
SEA BISTRO

Frédéric Hubig created Jeanne A and is also a manager at Astier. This new Jeanne is a sea bistro with a scaling bench, a large main room and a cozy basement. Try the fried smelt with ginger, the bass and seaweed tartare or the lobster sandwich in large or small portions. Prices are a pleasant surprise! The lunch set menu starts at 18€.

3, rue Mandar (2nd).
M° Sentier, Étienne Marcel.
Phone: 01 42 61 58 34. lamareejeanne.com

CLAMATO
LIKE BEYONCĒ

Bertrand Grébaut and Théo Pourriat are the genius chefs of Septime. They opened this second restaurant, and it specializes in seafood. It has a bucolic setting with a garden view, where the same inspired cuisine as Septime's is served: super fresh food with smart mixtures (urchin and carrot, octopus and kombu, red mullet and artichoke) and a daily menu. Even Beyoncé and Jay-Z come here! Lunch is around 35€.

80, rue de Charonne (11th). M° Charonne, Ledru-Rollin.
Phone: 01 43 72 74 53.
septime-charonne.fr

Clamato

CAFĒ DES ABATTOIRS
THE BEST MEAT

In the Rostang family, ask for Caroline and Sophie, and their meat counter! For two years we have been coming here to experience the best of butcher tradition: Black Angus steak, lamb shoulder, veal tartare. It is a delight for meat eaters and a good way to convert skeptics. Homemade condiments and light fries on the side. Their great idea was to create an aperitif set at the counter, with high-quality charcuterie. Lunch from 22€.

10, rue Gomboust (1st).
M° Pyramides.
Phone: 01 76 21 77 60.
cafedesabattoirs.com

Café des Abattoirs

VANESSA BRUNO
FASHION DESIGNER

HER RESTAURANT
VIRTUS
"This is a piece for four hands played by Chiho Kanzaki and Marcelo Martin di Giacomo, in which they explore the unmapped areas of a precise and refined cuisine."
8, rue Crozatier (12th)
M° Reuilly-Diderot
Phone: 09 80 68 08 08
virtus-paris.com

CANARD & CHAMPAGNE
BUBBLES!

This chic yet affordable restaurant combines the most festive of beverages and great little dishes. The Champagne served comes from small producers and costs only 8€ a glass. You can drink it while eating a delicious farm duck cooked at low temperature, then grilled. The setting is beautiful and classy, with leather marquetry on the ceilings. An appetizer and main course at 26€, 8€ for a dessert.

57, passage des Panoramas (2nd). M° Richelieu-Drouot, Grands Boulevards. Phone: 09 81 83 95 69.
canardetchampagne.com

Canard & Champagne

DILIA
A TUSCAN AIR

Michele Farnesi opened Dilia on the Ménilmontant hill, by the church. He is a young Tuscan chef trained in the best restaurants, for example, Thoumieux. Dinner is pricey, but it offers a series of small dishes made from exceptional produce. A smart choice is the lunch set menu or dinner set menu at the counter, which includes a pasta platter sold by weight (60, 90 or 120 grams for 11, 14 or 17€). When the sun is out, you can eat on the terrace with a view on the small square and feel like you are in Italy. Sitting in, lunch starts at 16€, dinner at 44€.

1, rue d'Eupatoria (20th).
M° Ménilmontant.
Phone: 09 53 56 24 14.
dilia.fr

Dilia

Pierre Sang

YANASE
CRAZY TOKYO
Sushi, sashimis, nigiris, teppanyakis...
Behind the counter, Mr. Osawa cooks
in front of his astounded customers,
mostly Japanese regulars. Good restaurants
are not rare in the 15th arrondissement,
but discreet Yanase is a well-known
place among Japan lovers.
For dinner, you can order a creative
sushi platter, to eat with chopsticks.
The trip to Tokyo is guaranteed,
with the customary Japanese
welcome and refinement.
Lunch starts at 20€, dinner at 35€.
75, rue Vasco-de-Gama (15th).
M° Balard, Porte de Versailles.
Phone: 01 42 50 07 20.

PIERRE SANG
SURPRISE MENU
The Top Chef contestant opened two
restaurants in Oberkampf. In the first one, you
can sit at the counter and look on as the cooks
put together a surprise menu. The creative
cooking changes each day. A few steps away
you can find his other restaurant, Atelier Pierre
Sang on Gambey, which also offers a mystery
menu, this time even fancier. The two locations
offer a surprising wine list.
Lunch starts at 20€, dinner at 39€ at
55, rue Oberkampf (11th). M° Parmentier, Oberkampf.
Phone: 09 67 31 96 80.
Lunch starts at 20€, dinner at 88€ at
6, rue Gambey (11th). M° Parmentier, Oberkampf.
Phone: 09 67 31 96 80.

ON A PLATTER
Les Commis and Cook Angels help
busy Parisians who like to cook.
Choose your menu in the morning
and receive the measured ingredients
that very night, peeled and cut, along
with a detailed step-by-step recipe.
Less than an hour later, it's ready!
Les Commis: Around 20€ per person for a full menu.
51, avenue Trudaine (9th).
M° Anvers, Pigalle.
Phone: 01 48 74 83 14.
lescommis.com
Cook Angels: Around 29€ per person for a full
menu or around 9.90€ per person for two dishes
per week with the subscription.
17, rue Saint-Sénoch (17th).
M° Pereire.
Phone: 09 81 73 28 69.
cookangels.com

Coretta

WORKING FOOD

Culinary laboratories CityChef and L'Étoile des Gourmets work everyday to deliver a chef's menu to your home, which you can order that very morning.

The dishes are packed in isothermal cases. They can be heated in the oven or in the skillet, depending on the instructions.

Set the table, and eat!

CityChef: Starts at 30€ per person for a full menu (for less than ten people) + 2€ delivery in Paris on citychef.fr

L'Étoile des Gourmets: Starts at 8€ for an appetizer, 15€ for a main course and 8€ for dessert + 10€ delivery on etoiledesgourmets.com

CORETTA
NEO-CLASSICAL

Chef Jean-François Pantaleon
cooks classics (sweetbreads, foie gras, scallops) in a luminous and welcoming setting, along with more surprising produce such as wild boar back. Sitting at the high tables on the first floor, those with a small appetite will be delighted with botanas, small tapas-like dishes. Lunch set menu with appetizer + main course or main course + dessert is 24.50€ and dinner from 35€.

151 bis, rue Cardinet (17th). M° Brochant.
Phone: 01 42 26 55 55.
restaurantcoretta.com

HAÏ KAÏ
LUXURY TAPAS

Close to the canal Saint-Martin,
Amélie Darvas creates refined and delicate recipes with market produce of the day. Every morning, she works on the dishes and tapas that you will find on the blackboard for lunch. In the evening, the carte blanche menu is a nine-course culinary delight. Lunch from 8€ to 35€. Tasting menu at 60€.

104, quai de Jemmapes (10th). M° Jacques Bonsergent, Gare de l'Est. Phone: 09 81 99 98 88. haikai.fr

Haï Kaï

Filomena

FILOMENA
SARDINIAN

Sardinian restaurants are rare −
all the more reason to try this one out.
Valentina Russino named her restaurant after
her grandmother to honor the family cooking.
In the kitchen, Marco Sechi modernizes island
classics. You will be delighted with the
culurgiones, potato ravioli with pecorino and
mint, or with the cuttlefish ink gnocchis, served
in large or small portions called cicchetti.
Prices for four cicchetti start at 40€.
9, rue Lobineau (6th). M° Mabillon.
Phone: 01 43 26 71 95.

PAPILLON
SUPER CHIC

Starred three times by the Michelin guide
when he was working with Alain Ducasse,
Christophe Saintagne has now opened his own
restaurant with a super chic decor perfectly
adapted to his "haute couture" creations: sunny-
side up egg with black truffle and pancetta,
roasted brill with olives and bitter herbs, citrus,
honey and Campari. 28€ for a lunch set menu,
55€ à la carte menu in the evening.
8, rue Meissonnier (17th). M° Wagram.
Phone: 01 56 79 81 88.
papillonparis.fr

MARTINE
DE RICHEVILLE
FOUNDER AT
MARTINE DE RICHEVILLE
RESHAPING

HER RESTAURANT
SOLA
"I love their French-Japanese fusion
food that is refined, light and creative.
Ask to be seated in the cellar with the
arch; it is surprising."
12, rue de l'Hôtel-Colbert (5th).
M° Maubert-Mutualité.
Phone: 09 65 01 73 68 for lunch
and 01 43 29 59 04 for dinner.

Papillon

LE SQUARE GARDETTE
DELICATELY YOURS

This restaurant has become the go-to place for many regular customers. The bargain-hunted decor with large chairs, retro wallpaper, hunting trophies on the walls and an English cottage look makes everyone feel at home. The food is delicate and well cooked by a twenty-five-year-old chef. The wine list is surprisingly affordable, allowing for a very reasonably priced dinner menu. What more could you ask for? 36€ dinner menu.

24, rue Saint-Ambroise (11th). M° Saint-Ambroise, Rue Saint-Maur. Phone: 01 43 55 63 07 and 01 85 15 23 28. squaregarette.com

LE TAXI JAUNE
LOCAL CUISINE AND WINE

This restaurant gives off a traditional-chic vibe. In charge is Otis Lebert, the managing world-travelling chef who makes up his menu based on his instinct and on his taste for game. Across the street, his boutique/grocery store/wine cellar displays bottles that are worth a taste: Mas d'Espanet, Romaneaux-Destezet, Leccia. 19€ for a lunch set menu. Around 50€ à la carte dinner.

13, rue Chapon (3rd). M° Arts et Métiers, Rambuteau. Phone: 01 42 76 00 40. restaurantletaxijaune.fr

Le Square Gardette

Clover

CLOVER
COOL JEAN-FRANÇOIS PIÈGE

To taste starred chef Jean-François Piège's high precision gastronomy, head toward this spot, less expensive than his Grand Restaurant on rue d'Aguesseau. At Clover, the master shows his talents in a bistro atmosphere, helped by the Japanese chef Shinya Usami. Taste the coconut milk lemongrass smoked herring or the light mashed turnips with a nasturtium sauce – Ideal! Around 60€ for dinner.

5, rue Perronet (7th). M° Rue du Bac, Saint-Germain-des-Prés. Phone: 01 75 50 00 05.

RESTAURANTS

ELMER
METICULOUS & DELICIOUS

This restaurant has everything: a luminous setting, large tables that can seat eight people so you can get to know your neighbors; a young talented chef Simon Horwitz that has already worked for two starred restaurants; and a caring team. In the kitchens, chefs are hard at work around a state-of-the-art grill and the greatest produce. The menu changes every day and its high standards extend even to the bread and butter, which are home-made. Around 50€ à la carte.

30, rue Notre-Dame-de-Nazareth (3rd).
M° Temple, République.
Phone: 01 43 56 22 95.

SARAH
ART DIRECTOR
AT COLETTE

HER RESTAURANT
VERJUS
"The chef Braden Perkins surprises me each time with an exceptional menu: creative, refined, fresh and always light. My little secret: Rent out their library room on the first floor for ten to twelve people, which has an amazing view on the Palais-Royal Theater."
52, rue de Richelieu (1st).
M° Pyramides, Bourse.
Phone: 01 42 97 54 40.
verjusparis.com

Elmer

PHĒBĒ
SAFE BET

In this 1900's decorated restaurant, seasonal and flavorful cuisine made with excellent produce is served. Try the squid wok appetizer with vegetables (and optional chorizo), then the roasted cod with ginger. To finish it off, there is a heated terrace – and a smile from the boss, Alain Liaigre. 21.50€ lunch menu.

190, rue de Courcelles (17th). M° Pereire.
Phone: 01 46 22 33 23.

Blue Valentine

BLUE VALENTINE
AMAZING TRIO

This great restaurant in the 11th is run by an amazing trio: Léna Balacco from the organic café Sésame, Simon Octobre from the Petit Cambodge and the oven maestro Terumitsu Saïto, who knows how to cook vegetables the way only Japanese chefs do. Bistro atmosphere and delicious small dishes: marinated whelk, broccoli cream, kohlrabi, citrus zest and froth, deer warm pate with fried foie gras, forester risotto, spinach, mushroom foam – how refined! Lunch menu starts at 21€, dinner menu starts at 41€.
13, rue de la Pierre-Levée (11th).
M° Goncourt, Parmentier.
Phone: 01 43 38 34 72.
bluevalentine-restaurant.fr

SATURNE
ORIGINAL MIXTURES

Watch out for this gem! The plain decor looks Nordic underneath the studio glass roof. On your plate, a party! It is a festival of flavors and original mixtures. For instance, the smoked beef tartare with celery in salty crust with an egg, Parmesan and Jerusalem artichoke chips, mussel turbot. You will want nothing more than to come back to this starred restaurant for more! 45€ lunch menu, 75€ six-course dinner menu.
17, rue Notre-Dame-des-Victoires (2nd). M° Bourse.
Phone: 01 42 60 31 90.
saturne-paris.fr

Ida

IDA
BIG ITALY

Somewhere between a trattoria and a gourmet restaurant, this is a great restaurant. Denny Imbroisi, who trained alongside Alain Ducasse at the Jules Verne, enjoys reinterpreting Italian classics. This Calabrian chef has an excellent reputation and was crowned "king of the carbonara" and he has published an Italian cookbook at editions Alain Ducasse. Lunch from 30€.
117, rue de Vaugirard (15th).
M° Falguière.
Phone: 01 56 58 00 02.

Saturne

CHEFS IN MY KITCHEN

On La Belle Assiette, nearly 600 professionals show their work in three to four menus. After having entered the date and place of your dinner, you can choose the chef and his menu, starting at 35€ per person for six people.

Phone: 01 76 34 00 34. labelleassiette.fr

Gare au Gorille

CHRISTOPHE MICHALAK
PASTRY CHEF

HIS RESTAURANTS
ATELIER VIVANDA + AKRAME

"Everything is divine at L'Atelier Vivanda and, right across from it, the Akrame restaurant! Akrame Benallal is my favorite chef – he is exceptionally gifted. I eat marvelously in these two restaurants. Don't miss out on his potato gratin and Parisian flan – to die for."

Atelier Vivanda : 18, rue Lauriston (16th). M° Kléber. Phone: 01 40 67 10 00.
ateliervivanda.com
Akrame : 19, rue Lauriston (16th). M° Kléber.
Phone: 01 40 67 11 16.
akrame.com

GARE AU GORILLE
A BREATHTAKING PLATE

Two former Septime chefs lead this restaurant, one of whom, Marc Cordonnier, learned to cook in the kitchens of Ze Kitchen Galerie and Alain Passard. The decoration is basic (white tiles, filament light-bulbs and wooden tables), yet the food is breathtaking – butternut velouté with grilled pig, raw veal with anchovy and sorrel – and enjoyed as full plates for lunch or tapas in the evening. 27€ Lunch menu.

68, rue des Dames (17th).
M° Rome.
Phone: 01 42 94 24 02.

BEST OF THE BEST

ARM YOURSELF WITH PATIENCE TO ACCESS THESE EXCELLENT RESTAURANTS THAT SUPPORT PARIS'S CULINARY REPUTATION

Ober Mamma

OBER MAMMA, EAST MAMMA AND **MAMMA PRIMI**
THE BEST OF ITALY

The best of Italy at cool prices — these three busy places refuse numerous customers every night. Pizzas from 12€.

107, boulevard Richard-Lenoir (11th). M° Oberkampf. Phone: 01 58 30 62 78.

133, rue du Faubourg-Saint-Antoine (11th). M° Ledru-Rollin. Phone: 01 43 41 32 15.

71, rue des Dames (17th). M° Rome.

bigmammagroup.com

New locations to come very soon!

LE RICHER AND
52 FAUBOURG-SAINT-DENIS
NEIGHBORHOOD BISTROS

Following up on the success of L'Office, Charles Compagnon acquired two new bistros, open non-stop from 8 a.m. to 12 p.m., where customers can wait for a table on the terrace. À la carte around 35€.

2, rue Richer (9th). M° Poissonnière, Bonne Nouvelle. lericher.com

52, rue du Faubourg-Saint-Denis (10th). M° Château d'Eau. faubourgstdenis.com

52 Faubourg-Saint-Denis

Frenchie

SEPTIME
A STAR IS BORN

His customary menu, creative cooking and attention to detail have earned Bertrand Grébaut a Michelin star for his beautifully designed bistro. We love the fact that you can book a table online. Lunch starts at 32€, carte blanche dinner at 70€. Bertrand has also opened La Cave, where you can taste and bring home his selection of wines and great produce.
Septime : 80, rue de Charonne (11th). M° Charonne.
Phone: 01 43 67 38 29.
La Cave : 3, rue Basfroi (11th). M° Charonne, Ledru-Rollin. Phone: 01 43 67 14 87.
septime-charonne.fr

Septime

FRENCHIE
FIVE TIME WALTZ

Gregory Marchand is a virtuoso cook whose five-course carte blanche menu attracts the entire city. His restaurant in rue du Nil is completely booked months in advance. We also love his wine bar, his cellar and café Frenchie To Go. 74€ menu.
5-6-9, rue du Nil (2nd). M° Sentier.
Phone: 01 40 39 96 19. frenchie-restaurant.com

LE SERVAN
PRECISE AND PERFECT

This restaurant is run by two gifted sisters. Tatiana and Katia Levha create plates with the same philosophy as at Septime, based on precision and perfection (Tatiana is chef Bertrand Grébaut's wife). Lunch starts at 25€, dinner menu at 60€.
32, rue Saint-Maur (11th). M° Père Lachaise.
Phone: 01 55 28 51 82.
leservan.com

LE CHATEAUBRIAND
AND **LE DAUPHIN**
GENIUS BISTRONOMY

No need to introduce Iñaki Aizpitarte and his two restaurants: these have given bistronomy prestige. If you are too impatient to taste the amazing Basque's cooking at the Chateaubriand, you can visit his cellar next door and order a daily special to go. Or you can try your luck at Le Dauphin.
Le Chateaubriand : 129, avenue Parmentier (11th). M° Goncourt. Phone: 01 43 57 45 95.
lechateaubriand.net.
Dinner menu is 70€.
Le Dauphin : 131, avenue Parmentier (11th). M° Goncourt.
Phone: 01 55 28 78 88. restaurantledauphin.net.
Tapas plates for about 9€. Lunch set menu from 15€.

GOING OUT

HAVING ONE OR TWO DRINKS, OR EVEN THREE **DRINKS,** IS NOT SO UNPLEASANT. NOR IS **DANCING, LAUGHING AND SINGING!**

TASTED AND
APPROVED

WINE BARS WHERE YOU CAN ENJOY DELICIOUS PLATTERS

ETNA
NATURAL WINES

Welcome to Etna, where you can discover natural wines selected by sommelier David Rougier (formerly at Meurice, Bristol and Akrame). In dimmed light, introduce yourself to surprising wines that go wonderfully well with the tapas. White truffled tarama and hazelnut burrata or Causses blue cheese from Quatrehomme with nuts – a great way to educate your palate! Glass from 7€, tapas from 6€.

33, rue Mazarine (6th). M° Mabillon, Odéon. Phone: 01 46 34 84 52. bar-etna.fr

Etna

Lucien la Chance

LUCIEN LA CHANCE
MORE THAN 100 SELECTIONS

The decor in this tapas bar, which was formerly a candy store, attracts attention with convex windows and beautiful woodwork. The drinks are great, too. The owner specializes in natural wines. More than 100 selections are paired with their refined dishes: cauliflower mousseline with lumpfish eggs, white port and pistachio foie gras carpaccio – they are all delicious! Glass from 5€, plate from 6€.

8, rue des Dames (17th). Place de Clichy, La Fourche. Phone: 09 73 52 07 14.

LA CAVE À MICHEL
TAPAS GALORE

This wine merchant with a Southern accent
welcomes you from 7 p.m. onward to nibble at small plates, like you would in Spain. Forget the charcuterie and cheese platters; eat tapas that range from eggs mayonnaise to boletus duck. Only three choices of white and red wine are available by the glass. The wine is always natural or fair trade, and the selection changes depending on the menu. Glass from 6€, small plate from 8€.

36, rue Sainte-Marthe (10th). M° Belleville, Colonel Fabien. Phone: 01 42 45 94 47.

LA BUVETTE DE CAMILLE
JOYOUS COUNTER

Retro decor from an old dairy shop,
zinc counter, a few tables and there you have it! Arrive early at Buvette de Camille to have a drink or play cards at the counter – it's worth it! Natural wines from small producers and luxury preserves, this place is perfect to grab a bite with friends. Glass from 5€, small plate from 6€.

67, rue Saint-Maur (11th). M° Rue St-Maur. Phone: 09 83 56 94 11.

LA CAVE DE BELLEVILLE
HORIZON GLASSES

Wine brought these three friends together
in an old leather factory, converted into a dining cellar, wine cellar and fine foods store. We go there to taste the well-priced wine of the month, sold by the bottle and that you can freely bring to the dining cellar. Adventurers can go on a wine world tour, from Spain to Argentina, through Bulgaria. To eat: Preserves from the sea, charcuterie and cheese. Glass from 4.50€, tapas from 5€.

51, rue de Belleville (19th). M° Pyrénées, Belleville. Phone: 01 40 34 12 95. lacavedebelleville.wordpress.com

La Buvette de Camille

Pássarito

PÁSSARITO
FRANCE-PORTUGAL

Pássarito is always full! The wine list presents French and Portuguese wines, the cheese and charcuterie platters promote the best producers of Lisbon, the decor is 100-percent azulejos and there is a children's area full of toys. Let's not forget the grocer's corner, as well as the family-produced olive oil, sold in bulk. You can order the bottle of wine of the month and drink it there, while having a 6€ platter.

10, rue Goncourt (11th). M° Goncourt.
Phone: 09 83 31 25 06.
passarito.com

CHEZ NOUS
JUST LIKE HOME

Chez Nous is like being at home: A warm place where you can drink natural wine (more than 150 selections on the list) on both sides of the counter. Watch the waiters work and enjoy a Chablis or Cheverny with homemade tapas (smoked fish or Iberian ham). Glass from 5€, plate from 5€. It is even open on Sunday evenings!

10, rue Dauphine (6th).
M° Saint-Michel.
Phone: 01 43 26 42 69.
cheznousparis.com

LE BARON ROUGE
AMAZING VALUE FOR MONEY

Everyone seems to know one another here. This landmark at Aligre market has been offering an amazing value for money for forty years. Their secret is that they buy large quantities of wine and let it ferment in their cellar. More than 45 selections are listed, among which an Ardèche merlot sold for 1.50€! The place is packed, especially on weekends, when people arrive to eat oysters and charcuterie on the terrace, sitting on barrels. Oyster platters for 7.50€, charcuterie or cheese platters for 7€.

1, rue Théophile-Roussel (12th). M° Ledru-Rollin, Faidherbe-Chaligny. Phone: 01 43 43 14 32.

Freddy's

En Vrac

EN VRAC
SIPS OF HAPPINESS

Every day until midnight, buy and taste natural wines kept in vats and served in reusable bottles. Whether in the large room or on the terrace, you can pair your favorite wine with the daily special, a soup or traditional produce such as sandwiches, sausage, or cheese. Bottles to go from 3.50€, daily special about 11.50€.

2, rue de l'Olive (18th). M° Marx Dormoy. Phone: 01 53 26 03 94. And two wine cellars (9th and 10th). vinenvrac.fr

GO HOME IN A PRIVATE CAR

Chauffeur-Privé, CinqS, LeCab, Joseff, SnapCar, Marcel, Uber, these smartphone apps have it all: instant booking, comfortable cars, automatic payments and priviledged attention, depending on the service booked.

chauffeur-prive.com, cinq-s.com, joseff.fr, lecab.fr, marcel.cab, snapcar.com and uber.com

FREDDY'S
THE WORLD IN A BOTTLE

Thought up by the team at the Semilla, this spot offers a beautiful selection of small producer wines, good hard cider, grilled tapas, yakitoris and the delightful creations of Eric Trochon, Meilleur Ouvrier de France, such as cauliflower tabbouleh and watermelon ceviche. The bonus is the welcoming atmosphere at lunch and dinner time. Glass from 5€, small plates from 6€.

54, rue de Seine (6th). M° Saint-Germain-des-Prés, Mabillon. No phone. No reservations.

COCKTAIL
PARTY
BARS WITH SURPRISING DRINKS AND DESIGNS

Pas de Loup

PAS DE LOUP
DOUBLE IT

In this bar, cocktails and food are wonderfully paired. In a Scandinavian-inspired decor, two adjoining rooms each have a bar and set a different mood. On the one hand, there is the kitchen and high tables. On the other, mixology and a cozy atmosphere. We love the creative cocktails with a single price (12€), and the pairing suggestions that offer gourmet platters to best accompany the drinks.

108, rue Amelot (11ᵗʰ). M° Filles du Calvaire.
pasdeloupparis.com

COPPERBAY
IN VOGUE

This is the opposite of a muted cocktail bar – here, a huge window lets the light into a room with a sumptuous copper chandelier and sailing ropes. Order a cocktail at the main table after carefully studying the menu and its selection of flavors, and watch the pros at work. A gold star for the different containers used for each recipe, and the prices that range from 10 to 12€.

5, rue Bouchardon (10ᵗʰ).
M° Strasbourg Saint-Denis, Jacques Bonsergent.
copperbay.fr

LE SYNDICAT
FRENCH CONNECTION

A trashy exterior, a rough interior and luxury mixology: this is the recipe used in this place, which actively promotes French liquors. Romain Le Mouellic and Sullivan Doh toured the country to find the best alcohol. The list is an initiatic journey with tasting glasses of pure creations and revisited English classics. Around 13€.

51, rue du Faubourg-Saint-Denis (10ᵗʰ).
M° Château d'Eau, Strasbourg Saint-Denis.
syndicatcocktailclub.com

Le Syndicat

LAVOMATIC
BEATING DRUMS

Let's meet at the Laundromat! The door to the dryer leads to a dark staircase and a friendly bar with large couches, high tables to stand at and eat, and swinging chairs. On the menu, you will find some cocktails with surprising ingredients, such as horseradish or salmon-infused Stolichnaya vodka. Small plates are also available for small appetites. Cocktails from 9 to 12€.

30, rue René-Boulanger (10th). M° République.
lavomatic.paris

Lavomatic

BEER, BEER AND MORE BEER

La Fine Mousse is the place for beer drinkers. This draft beer bar offers no less than 150 bottled beers and 20 beer pumps that necessitate a whole cold chamber, the only one in the world. Each week, dozens of beers change, and brewers are regularly invited to present their production. **About 8-fluid-ounce draft from 4.50€.**

6, avenue Jean-Aicard (11th).
M° Rue St-Maur.
Phone: 01 48 06 40 94.
lafinemousse.fr

LE BARANAAN
THE ROAD TO INDIA

There is more to this lassi, chai and fresh juice bar than meets the eye. Go through the back door and discover a train-like Prohibition cocktail bar! Pictures of Kerala are shown on screens while you pick you seat and beverage – Pajma, Dura Dura, Indira's Affair... from 10 to 12€. Hungry? Naans from 3 to 7€ are made on the spot and cooked in a disco-ball-shape oven.

7, rue du Faubourg-Saint-Martin (10th).
M° Strasbourg Saint-Denis.
Phone: 01 40 38 97 57.
baranaan.com

Le Baranaan

Le Mary Celeste

LE MARY CELESTE
DRINK IN A MARITIME SETTING

Night owls meet here to taste seasonal cocktails (12 or 13€) along with sharing plates for two or three people (from 7 to 12€) or an oyster platter with the amount and type of oysters you want (from 1.80€ for one). The setting is luminous, and the atmosphere festive. If you are coming in a large group, book a table online beforehand.

1, rue Commines (3rd).
M° Saint-Sébastien Froissart, Filles du Calvaire.
Phone: 09 80 72 98 83.
lemaryceleste.com

L'IMPASSE
COZY LOFT

In the heart of Oberkampf, this huge artist's loft is hidden in a one-way street, on the first floor of an old factory. Secluded from the festive noises of rue Oberkampf, take a seat in the comfortable chairs and couches bought at Emmaüs. On the list are about twenty different natural wines, cocktails and Basque charcuterie platters from Ospital house. Glass from 4.50€, platter from 17€.

4, cité Griset (11th).
M° Ménilmontant, Parmentier.
Phone: 09 52 53 04 19.

COCKTAILS FOR BEGINNERS

Do you dream of organizing a cocktail party, but lack the mixology knowledge? Head to La Cave à Cocktail. They provide made-to-order cocktails with fresh fruit and vegetables, with or without alcohol, to take out in a chic black bottle (starts at 20€ virgin, 35€ with alcohol).

62, rue Greneta (2nd). M° Sentier, Étienne Marcel. Phone: 09 54 55 50 00.
cave-cocktail.com

BALLROOM
BASEMENT MELODY

It is hard to pick just one place among the different cocktail bars managed by the handsome guys of the Expérimental Group. This one is located underneath their two popular restaurants, Fish Club and Beef Club (with direct access to the bar), and offers live music every Thursday night. From 13€ for a cocktail.

58, rue Jean-Jacques-Rousseau (1st).
M° Les Halles, Étienne Marcel.
Phone: 09 52 52 89 34.

LULU WHITE
JAZZY COOL

This place pays homage to an icon of 1910 New Orleans. The team at Little Red Door (3rd) moved from one scandalous place to the next, creating here an Art nouveau setting with jazz and swing airs mixed with electro. On the menu, you will find absinthe, cognac and bourbon in skillfully dosed cocktails, from 9 to 13€.

12, rue Frochot (9th).
M° Pigalle.
luluwhite.bar

UC-61
UNDERWATER DECOR

This micro cocktail bar is hidden behind a military front and offers an underwater decor. You have to ring a bell to get in. The barmaid Anaïs will welcome you into a spot where nothing is left to chance, from the bargain-hunted vintage phone to the rusty paint. Numerous refined creations are on the menu, including La Délicatesse, a vodka-based cocktail with limoncello, fresh mint and lime (14€).

4, rue de l'Arc-de-Triomphe (17th).
M° Charles de Gaulle Étoile, Ternes.
Phone: 01 40 68 70 60.
uc-61.com

Lulu White

LET'S ALL MEET AT
THE BISTRO!

NEIGHBORHOOD BAR, GAME BAR, BEAUTY BAR, MUSIC JOINT : ALL OF THESE PLACES HAVE A LITTLE SOMETHING EXTRA

LES NIÇOIS
WITH AN ACCENT

The French Riviera imported into Paris – what a neat idea! With pétanque and foosball downstairs, pissaladière and pan bagnat on the menu, rosé and tapenade on the grocer's shelves, to eat in or take out – we're crazy about Les Niçois!

7, rue Lacharrière (11th).
M° Saint-Ambroise, Rue St-Maur.
Phone: 09 84 16 55 03.
lesnicois.com

DE L'AMITIĒ CAFĒ
WITHOUT A FUSS

First, there is the decor of randomly aligned tables made from cylinders and ropes, recycled chairs and armchairs. Then, there is the small fuss-free menu, which offers charcuterie, burgers and pitchers of wine. Finally, there is the boss, who will not hesitate to turn up the music like in a club. All of this makes for a well-named friendly bar that is full every night when the neighbors decide to meet.

22, rue des Vignoles (20th). M° Buzenval, Avron.
Phone: 01 43 79 83 14.

LES BELLES COPINES

Les Belles Copines is a two-in-one all women's bar. During the day or at night, you can go there for a drink, a bite, a manicure, a mini-massage or a make-up session. This place can also be booked for private beauty parties.

2, rue Lemercier (17th).
M° Place de Clichy, La Fourche.
Phone: 09 83 66 48 39.
lesbellescopines.fr

LES PĒRES POPULAIRES
SHORT COFFEE, SHORT PRICES

This is the best value for money in the city for food and drinks. The Pères Pop, as it is affectionately known, wanted to fight the trend of expensive bars, and they offer an incredible list, starting with the 1€ coffee made by small producers on one of the best machines. From morning to evening, the offer is always beyond reproach, from the organic lunch set menu (16€ for appetizer, main course and dessert) to the aperitif.

46, rue de Buzenval (20th).
M° Buzenval.
Phone: 01 43 48 49 22.

Walrus

WALRUS
BARTENDER, A RECORD!

Julie David and Caroline Kutter-Vinrich worked at Fnac before opening this record counter. Look through the boxes where records mingle: new or old, pop, indie rock, folk. Machines let you listen to 500 albums out of the 3,000 available. Have a coffee, wine glass or draft beer at the bar or in the main room.

34 ter, rue de Dunkerque (10th).
M° Barbès-Rochechouart, Gare du Nord.
Phone: 01 45 26 06 40.
the-walrus.fr

LET'S **DANCE!**

PLACES TO PARTY, WORRY FREE

BRASSERIE BARBĒS
RETRACTABLE ROOF

At the foot of the Barbès metro station, this is the ideal place for a friendly dinner on the first floor, drinks in the winter garden with a retractable roof on the second floor, then dancing on the third. This place opens at 7 p.m. every night and provides a cozy atmosphere. From 11 p.m., clubbing starts with diverse DJ sets that last until 2 a.m.

2, boulevard Barbès (18th).
M° Barbès-Rochechouart.
Phone: 01 42 64 52 23.
brasseriebarbes.com

Brasserie Barbès

Le Riviera

LE RIVIERA
AFTER WORK

This cool place with a Gunther Love and Stuntman Dave (resident DJ) program has a strong concept: early dancing. At Riviera, created by the Niçois team, cocktails start at 8 p.m., the dance floor opens at 10 p.m. and bed time is at 2 a.m.! A small menu offers finger food: beef and cheddar or ham sandwiches and thyme-flavored house fries... This place will remain open until March 2017, or even later if it works well. We hope they can keep going!

2, villa Gaudelet (11th).
M° Parmentier.
Phone: 09 82 33 62 39.

Pavillon Puebla

ROSA BONHEUR
FRIENDLY ATMOSPHERE
We come here for the fun dance-hall atmosphere on Buttes-Chaumont (until midnight) or on its barge on the Seine, at the foot of Alexandre-III bridge (until 2 a.m.). The easy-going ambience and music are appealing. Early in the evening, you can try the tapas and dishes from Camargue and, on the barge, a made-to-order pizza, hot from the oven on the quay.

Port des Invalides (7th).

M° Invalides.

Phone: 01 47 53 66 92.

Parc des Buttes-Chaumont. 2, avenue de la Cascade (19th). M° Botzaris. Phone: 01 42 00 00 45.

rosabonheur.fr

PAVILLON PUEBLA
TO DANCE
Hidden in the Buttes-Chaumont park, this Italian restaurant and festive bar is the fourth location opened by the team at Perchoir, who are behind the famous rooftop bar on the last two stories of a garage (14, rue Crespin-du-Gast, 11th). We love the countryside ambience, the two terraces and wild-chic decor. On Sundays, "La Guinchette" is a kids'party with lunch and entertainment – and peace for the parents!

39, avenue Simon-Bolivar (19th).

M° Buttes Chaumont. Phone: 01 42 39 34 20.

leperchoir.tv

Rosa Bonheur

LE BAR Ā BULLES
BEFORE GOING OUT
Found right above La Machine du Moulin Rouge, the Sinny&Ooko collective has opened this bar/restaurant/garden/patio with an eclectic program. Party animals meet here before going out on Fridays and Saturdays until 2 a.m. Regulars go from this hidden space to the club; both share the same program, with a different mood on every floor.

4 bis, cité Véron (18th).

M° Blanche.

Phone: 01 53 41 88 86.

barabulles.paris

ISABEL MARANT
FASHION DESIGNER

HER CLUB
LA MANO
"I go there to dance.
This place is great to party,
and listen to music ... with a great
Mexican atmosphere."
10, rue Papillon (9th). M° Poissonnière, Cadet.
Phone: 09 67 50 50 37.

HOTELS

WHETHER TO SLEEP OR PLAY, THESE PLACES HAVE **IMPECCABLE TASTE**.

NOTHING HOLDS BACK THE **NIGHT**

HOTELS FOR STAYING JUST THE NIGHT, OR PERHAPS EVEN LESS (IF SYMPATHETIC)

Hôtel Henriette

HŌTEL HENRIETTE
GUEST ROOMS

This place is like a second home!
Vanessa manages the Henriette. She used to be a fashion designer, and thought up and decorated this charming hotel entirely herself by bargain hunting objects and furniture. The result: thirty-two original rooms, all of them different, with walls of wood, stonework or filled with color, fluffy blankets. Single room from 89€, double from 109€.

9, rue des Gobelins (13th). M° Les Gobelins.
Phone: 01 47 07 26 90.
hotelhenriette.com

HŌTEL DES GRANDES ĒCOLES
PARISIAN GARDEN

In the middle of the Latin Quarter,
this hotel is a haven in the center of a 1,200-square-yard garden. The classic decor in this old family pension is far from trendy design. This countryside ambience in Paris is charming – listen to the birds singing while having breakfast. From 135€ for a one-to-two-person room.

75, rue du Cardinal-Lemoine (5th).
M° Cardinal Lemoine, Place Monge.
Phone: 01 43 26 79 23.
hotel-grandes-ecoles.com

Hôtel des Grandes Écoles

HÔTEL PARIS BASTILLE BOUTET
LUMINOUS 5 STARS

This is the first 5-star hotel in eastern Paris, for which Sofitel group restored an old wood factory (also a former chocolate factory) right next to Faubourg Saint-Antoine. This beautiful industrial building has eighty luminous rooms – ten with a terrace – a pool, a spa and a fitness center. From 199€ per room.

22-24, rue Faidherbe (11ᵗʰ).
M° Faidherbe-Chaligny.
Phone: 01 40 24 65 65.
sofitel.com

VILLA DU SQUARE
VIEW ON LE CORBUSIER

This guesthouse was tastefully thought up by a couple of aesthetes, and is located in a private 1920's mansion next door to two Le Corbusier-designed villas. There are five spacious rooms with a garden view. We feel at home here – even better! From 150€ for a double room breakfast included.

26, rue Raffet (16ᵗʰ). M° Jasmin.
Phone: 01 71 72 91 33.
villadusquare.com

HÔTEL COSMOS
GOOD DEAL

Located in the trendy Oberkampf neighborhood, hotel Cosmos has many assets: spacious rooms, simple decor, a substantial breakfast, warm welcome. We understand why the clientele is often made up of regulars. This is a great place, so make sure you book early! Single room from 66€, double from 72€.

36, rue Jean-Pierre-Timbaud (11ᵗʰ). M° Parmentier.
Phone: 01 43 57 25 88.
comos-hotel-paris.com

EASY LUGGAGE

With 2kids 1bag, you no longer have to carry heavy luggage and take care of the kids!
You can rent a stroller, baby bed, high chair and bath for the time of your trip, and have them delivered. From 2.79€ per day for a stroller. Airport delivery available. Isn't life beautiful?

Book on the website 2kids1bag.com

HÔTEL EDGAR
SWEET DREAMS

Originally a clothing manufacture in Le Sentier, this building has been transformed into a charming hotel. The rooms were designed by friends of the owner (an art director, a photographer and a sculptor) and each room is different from the next: "Ébène Rock," "La Cabane de nos grands-parents" (our grandparents' cabin) and "Milagros," which features a cool revisited Texan style. The restaurant offers seafood and is the perfect place for breakfast or an aperitif, with a contemporary decor in the main room and a terrace. From 155€ per night in the off season.

31, rue d'Alexandrie (2ⁿᵈ). M° Sentier, Strasbourg Saint-Denis. Phone: 01 40 41 05 19.
Restaurant: 01 40 41 05 69.
edgarparis.com

Hôtel Edgar

Hôtel de Nell

HÔTEL DE NELL
CHIC IN BED

In a calm little street, Jean-Michel Wilmotte designed this five-star hotel from Charm & More Hotels. The thirty-three rooms are very luminous and terribly chic: massive oak, marble, Japanese baths (only in the "Luxury" category). On the first floor, the restaurant, La Régalade Conservatoire, offers the bistronomy cuisine of Bruno Doucet. From 200€ per night.

7-9, rue du Conservatoire (9ᵗʰ).
M° Grands Boulevards.
Phone: 01 44 83 83 60.
hoteldenell.com

HŌTEL PANACHE
ART NOUVEAU SLEEP

Near the Grands Boulevards, this seven-story hotel is full of panache! Adrien Gloagen asked architect Dorothée Meilichzon to renovate this building, just like he did for hotel Paradis. The result is forty Art nouveau rooms, all different. Note that breakfast and desserts are served partly by Noglu, and that lunch and dinner are orchestrated by David Lanher (the chef at Racines). From 130€ per night .

1, rue Geoffroy-Marie (9th).
M° Grands Boulevards, Le Peletier.
Phone: 01 47 70 85 87.
hotelpanache.com

HŌTEL ĒMILE
MODERN SLEEP

This modern hotel in the Marais offers twenty-nine rooms, including a few singles. It was designed by Alfred Klopper (who also created the inspired scenography of hotel Amour). The graphic decor mixes printed motifs on walls and drapes, and the white tiles in the bathrooms are reminiscent of Parisian subway stations. From 150€ for a double room, breakfast included.

2, rue Malher (4th). M° Saint-Paul.
Phone: 01 42 72 76 17.
hotelemile.com

ECTOR, THE PARKING VALET

Book a valet on the app or website Ector, who will pick up your car at Parisian airports as well as several train stations. The valet will take your keys and park your car in reduce-priced parking spaces at a distance from your location. 45€ for a weekend.
Available on the App Store and Google Play.
ectorparking.com

C.O.Q

LES PIAULES
YOUNG AND FESTIVE

This youth hostel in Belleville is full, night and day. Out of the 162 beds, young travellers favor the twenty-seven dormitories (capacity of four, six or eight people), while couples enjoy one of the seven double rooms, or treat themselves to a luxury rooftop room. On the first floor, a festive and multinational ambience reigns at the bar! From 25€ for a dormitory bed, and 90€ for a double room.

59, boulevard de Belleville (11th).
M° Couronnes.
Phone: 01 43 55 09 97.
lespiaules.com

Les Piaules

C.O.Q
FRIENDLY NIGHTS

Close to Place d'Italie, this original building mixes the codes of hotel trade with those of guest houses. Their ambition is to create a friendly place, open to the neighborhood. We love the winter garden, the designed or bargain-hunted objects chosen by home stylists, and the motif tiles called "pied-de-coq" in French — homage to this place's name, which is an acronym for Community of Quality. From 120€ per night.

15, rue Édouard-Manet (13th). M° Place d'Italie, Campo-Formio. Phone: 01 45 86 35 99.

coq-hotel-paris.com

FIVE TO SEVEN

Do you dream of an intimate time with your lover or your husband, without risking to be interrupted by the children? Go to Dayuse, where you can book a room for a few hours and at the last minute, with heavy reductions (up to 75-percent off).

Available on the App Store and Google Play.
Phone: 01 84 16 15 69.
dayuse.fr

HOTELS

PARIS OFF SEINE
FLOATING HOTEL

This floating hotel that opened last summer is moored close to the Austerlitz train station, by the Cité de la Mode et du Design. This architectural prowess is made up of two hulls, fifty-eight rooms, including four suites. We particularly love the bar, sun lounge, small pool and, of course, the view of the Seine! From 160€ per night in a double-room.

20-22, port d'Austerlitz (13th).
M° Gare d'Austerlitz.
offparisseine.com

Paris Off Seine

HÔTEL PROVIDENCE
DO NOT DISTURB…

Close to the porte Saint Martin and the busy boulevards, this hotel is located in a calm pedestrian street with a tree-lined terrace. The bar and restaurant on the first floor are open to anyone. The eighteen rooms upstairs all have a bar and a decor with refined details: graphic wallpaper, velvet fabric, etc. From 190€ per night.

90, rue René-Boulanger (10th).
M° Strasbourg Saint-Denis.
Phone: 01 46 34 34 04.
hotelprovidenceparis.com

ALIZA JABĒS
FOUNDER OF
NUXE COSMETICS

HER HOTEL
HÔTEL BACHAUMONT
"I love this hotel for its Dorothée Meilichzon design, its cool atmosphere underneath the glass roof, its kitchen and delicious cocktails."
18, rue Bachaumont (2nd). M° Sentier.
Phone: 01 81 66 47 00.
hotelbachaumont.com

Hôtel Providence

A WEEKEND IN THE **COUNTRY**

A SELECTION OF HOTELS AND GUESTHOUSES, LESS THAN 2 HOURS AWAY FROM PARIS

Étape du Cerf-Volant

MAISON PRAIRIE BONHEUR
AHOY FROM THE CASTLE

Only 30 minutes away from Paris, this countryside house in the Haute Vallée de Chevreuse natural regional park offers five rooms, a six-person guest-house and an outdoor jacuzzi at 99° Fahrenheit (costs extra). This house is located near the forest, and not far from the château de Breteuil, the château de Versailles and the Vaux-de-Cernay abbey, is perfect for walks and cultural visits. From 80€ per night .

6, chemin des Patissiaux, Magny-les-Hameaux (78).
Phone: 01 30 44 26 08.
chambres-hotes-prairie-bonheur.com

ÉTAPE DU CERF-VOLANT
CABIN IN THE FOREST

There's nothing better to energize than a short stay in a wood cabin, lost in the Rambouillet forest. With friends or family, you can choose between three cabins in this eco-friendly guesthouse. All cabins are equipped with a kitchen with shelves full of organic produce, a living room, a shower, etc. From 210€ per night .

Route de la Chesnaye, Le Mesle, Adainville (78).
Phone: 01 34 87 15 50. le-cerfvolant-rambouillet.com

LES HAUTES SOURCES
WELCOME TO THE FAMILY

In the middle of a small village in Eure, this beautiful building has three guest rooms, a family house and a treehouse. The espalier park offers an exceptional view of the countryside, the pool (open May to October) and the tennis court. From 120€ per night .

32, rue Roederer, Ménilles (27).
Phone: 06 72 84 91 89.
les-hautes-sources.fr

La Grange Saint-Martin

Tiara Château Hôtel Mont Royal Chantilly

TIARA CHĀTEAU HŌTEL
MONT ROYAL CHANTILLY
CASTLE LIFE

**This is the perfect place to live like
a princess** in one of the 108 rooms and
luxurious suites. Sip a cocktail by the fireplace.
Treat yourself to a gourmet dinner.
Receive a Carita treatment at the spa.
And, until 10 p.m., take a dip in the indoor pool.
From 260€ per night .
Route de Plailly, La Chapelle-en-Serval (60).
Phone: 03 44 54 50 50.
montroyal-chantilly.tiara-hotels.com

LA GRANGE SAINT-MARTIN
IN A TREE HOUSE

This former farm from Brie offers
five guest rooms and four cabins in the trees,
in the middle of its 37-acre prairie.
Breakfast by the wood burner, stylish and
welcoming rooms, cabins to play
Robinson Crusoe with a chic aperitif pic-nic
(from 30€) –Bravo!
From 120€ per night .
39, rue de la Coudre, Fontaine-le-Port (77).
Phone: 06 87 49 24 40.
lagrangesaintmartin.com

LA MINOTTE
FIDELITY HOST

This pretty town house has five chic and
cozy guest rooms, a beautiful outdoor pool
and a steam room where you can treat
yourself to a horsehair glove and black soap
treatment (85€). La Minotte offers a table
d'hôte during the week (37€).
From 140€ per night .
7, rue de Versailles, Monfort-l'Amaury (78).
Phone: 06 23 56 74 92.
laminotte.fr

Les Hautes Sources

La Dîme de Giverny

LA DÎME DE GIVERNY
IMPRESSIONIST IMPRESSIONS

547 yards from Claude Monet's garden, this guest house has a lovely courtyard and beautiful terrace. It mixes contemporary renovation and chic recycling with five rooms and two cottages with different ambiences. From 135€ per night.

2, rue de la Dîme, Giverny (27).
Phone: 06 20 83 28 90.
ladimedegiverny.com

LE JARDIN DES PLUMES
WAVE TO MONET

Eric Guerin's hotel-restaurant is located inside a charming tree-lined garden, a street away from busy Giverny. Two moods alternate in the rooms: the classical-chic mood of the House, and the modern and wooden mood of the Studio. From Wednesday to Sunday, eat at the one-Michelin star restaurant. From 180€ per night and 17 to 22€ for breakfast.

1, rue du Milieu, Giverny (27).
Phone: 02 32 54 26 35.
jardindesplumes.fr

D'UNE ÎLE
TINY PRETTY VILLAGE

In the middle of Perche, the guest rooms hosted by this young couple form a tiny village surrounded by five buildings. A total of nine rooms with a tasteful recycling decor can welcome two to six guests. The Super Suite was originally a house remade into three cabins for two. From 105€ per night + 9€ for breakfast.

Domaine de Launay, lieu-dit Launay, Rémalard (61).
Phone: 02 33 83 01 47.
duneile.com

LE DOMAINE DES EVIS
OPEN FARM

This former fortified farm includes a main house with five adult rooms, two children's rooms, a living room, a veranda – and an independent house for seven. You can eat all your meals here, treat yourself at the spa, take yoga classes or enjoy the outdoor heated pool. From 120€ per night.

Domaine des Evis, La Chapelle-Fortin (28).
Phone: 02 37 37 57 78.
domaine-des-evis.com

Le Domaine des Evis

Le Château des Moyeux

LE CHÂTEAU DES MOYEUX
PINCH ME, I'M DREAMING

In this gorgeous historical building, you will be treated like a princess in one of the four guest rooms. You can swim under a glass roof in 82° Fahrenheit water, and take a walk in the 92-acre park that contains a small chapel. A little off the beaten track, two cottages can welcome six to ten people. From 150€ per night.
Les Moyeux, La Chapelle-Rablais (77).
Phone: 01 64 08 49 51.
chateau-des-moyeux.com

La Ferme des Isles

LA FERME DES ISLES
A DIP IN THE EURE

Donkeys, sheep, chicken, geese and ducks... This pretty guesthouse offers a true nature experience with the possibility to swim in the Eure River, which flows across the 20-acre domain. The five rooms have character and all offer a different mood, and the food at the table d'hôte is made from home-grown produce. From 98€ per night.
7, chemin des Isles, Autheuil-Authouillet (27).
Phone: 02 32 36 66 14.
lafermedesisles.com

CHILDREN

THE CITY PROVIDES FOR **THE LITTLE ONES** – AND THE **OLDER ONES** TOO!

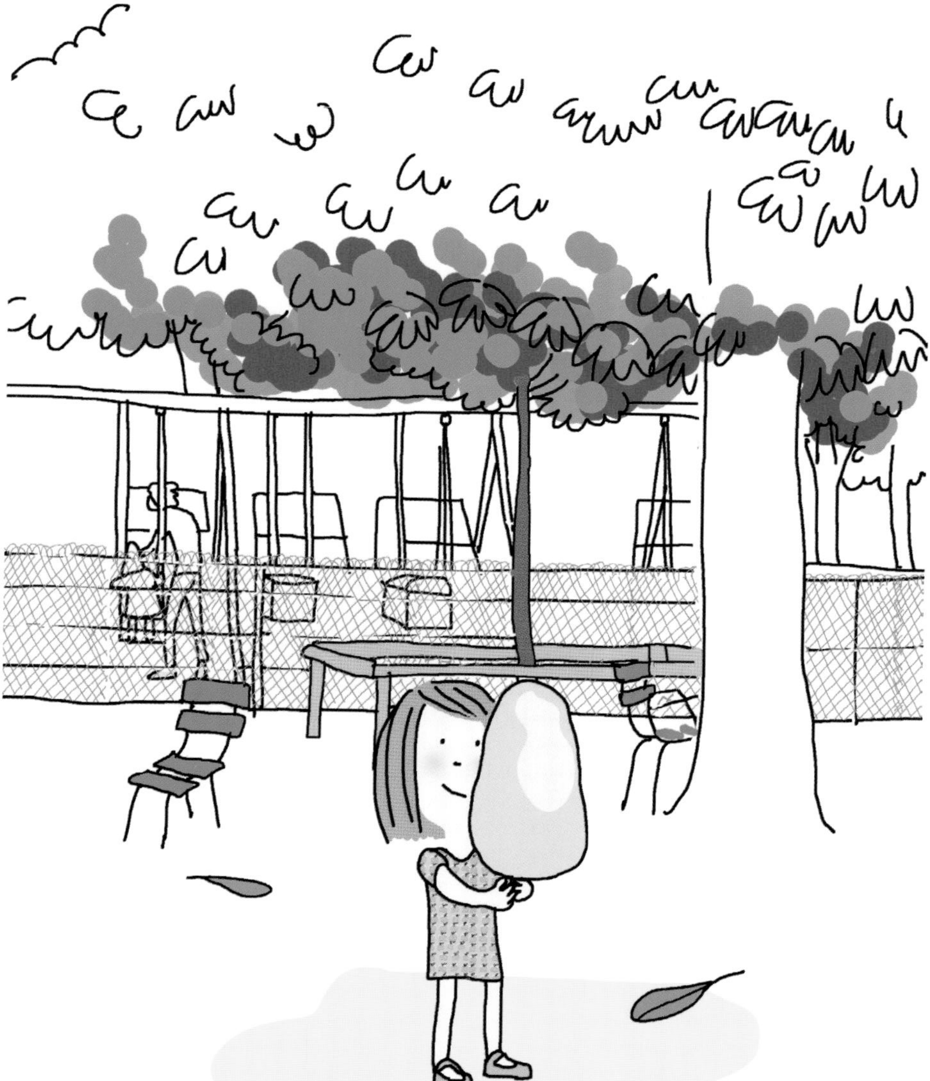

BABY'S
PLACES

THE BEST CHILD-FRIENDLY PLACES IN PARIS

Mombini

MOMBINI
PURE JOY!

This joyous and colorful place offers a shop, café, workshops and discoveries.
Enter through the boutique for children and adults, which includes numerous decor accessories and toys selected for their concept and design. In the back, a teahouse serves tarts or quiches for lunch, and there is a small play area. Upstairs, workshops are open to children and parents.
22, rue Gerbert (15th). M° Vaugirard.
Phone: 01 73 70 62 31.
mombini.com

Poule Mouillette

POULE MOUILLETTE
PUBLIC OR PRIVATE?
This is a boutique and teahouse to share.
On the first floor, smart toys, pretty birth gifts or homemade pastries will please adults.
The space upstairs is used either for workshops (musical awakening for babies, story-telling or baby sign language) and birthday parties, or as a cozy teahouse. You can rent out the entire space on Sundays.
13, rue des Récollets (10th).
M° Gare de l'Est.
Phone: 09 83 22 32 17.
poulemouillette.fr

UN AIR DE FAMILLE
WAIT YOUR TURN!

This space is booked for children and parents – albeit not at the same time. During the day, workshops are taught for babies and future moms. After school, artistic and sporting activities take place until 7:30 p.m. Then, until 10 p.m., the place is cleared for adults: cardio gym, strengthening exercises, shiatsu massage. During the week, this place also serves lunch.

26, rue du Château-Landon (10ᵗʰ). M° Louis Blanc.
Phone: 01 42 05 01 24.
air-de-famille.fr

SUPER CAFÉ
IS EVERYONE HAPPY?

This super café earns its name. You can come here at all times with your troop. While the parents eat dinner, children can watch a movie, climb inside the book- and cushion-filled cabin, or have fun in the game room. The menu offers dishes made with local produce, often organic. When the sun is out, deckchairs are put out on the terrace. Adult menu is 13€, kid menu is 7€.

16, rue de Fontarabie (20ᵗʰ).
M° Alexandre Dumas, Maraîchers.
Phone: 09 81 94 44 98.

Un Air de Famille

SUPER Café

BABY SITTING INCLUDED

You can get someone to watch over your children while you treat yourself! Mum & Babe came up with a great idea: While mom gets her hair done, a massage or a wax, the children can have fun in the game room, with or without a chaperone, depending on their age (3, rue Keller, 11ᵗʰ. M° Ledru-Rollin, Voltaire. Phone: 01 43 38 83 55. and 79, rue des Entrepreneurs, 15ᵗʰ. M° Commerce. Phone: 01 45 75 80 53.).

Another good place is Jolies Mamans, a beauty salon that provides a baby-sitter and even aqua cycling classes to get fit (10, rue du Faubourg-Poissonnière, 10ᵗʰ. M° Bonne-Nouvelle. Phone: 09 83 68 00 25.).

mumandbabe.fr and joliesmamans.com

GIFTS
FROM MOM!

DECOR, TOYS AND FASHION: PLACES THAT ATTRACT PARENTS AND KIDS

BALOUGA
BACK TO THE FUTURE

Véronique specializes in vintage furniture for kids, and recently extended her selection to include contemporary decor. Her priorities are still beauty, utility and functionality. A lot of furniture can be found here, along with wallpaper, construction toys (made from wood and cardboard), decor items.

1, rue Notre-Dame-de-Nazareth (3rd).
M° République, Temple.
Phone: 01 42 74 01 49.
balouga.com

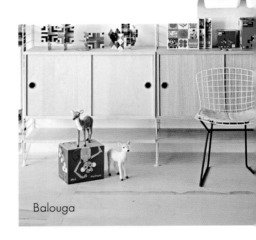

Balouga

SMALLable

SMALLABLE
IN REAL LIFE

This online landmark in children's fashion and decor opened a superb Parisian shop. In a 360-square-yard loft, more than 450 brands are featured. With so many options, from the birth gift or skateboard to displays of women's clothes, you may find it difficult to choose. You can also place an order in the store and have everything delivered to your home.

81, rue du Cherche-Midi (6th). M° Vaneau, Saint-Placide.
Phone: 01 40 46 01 15.
smallable.com

Centre Commercial Kids

CENTRE COMMERCIAL KIDS
FAIR-TRADE PLEASURES
This is the place for eco-friendly parents.
Just like the concept store located a
few streets away, this boutique exclusively for
children from birth to fourteen years old sells
clothes, accessories, toys and decor objects
made from natural and organic fabric, if
possible made in France. Workshops take
place on Wednesday afternoons.
22, rue Yves-Toudic (10th).
M° Jacques Bonsergent, République.
Phone: 01 42 06 23 81.
centrecommercial.cc/kids

UBE ULE
KEEP ON ROLLIN', KIDS!
In this Aladdin's cave of a store,
you will find a selection of gorgeous clothes
for babies and children (up to six years old)
from unknown and fun brands like Modéerska
Huset, Anïve for the minors or Gardner and
the Gang. Plenty of retro toys and cuddly toys
are displayed as well, each cuter than the next!
This is the ideal place to shop for birth or
birthday presents.
59, rue Condorcet (9th).
M° Anvers, Saint-Georges.
Phone: 01 45 26 93 63.
ube-ule.com

BY SOPHIE
LIGHT LINE
This is a homemade clothing line for moms,
with simple shapes cut from leftover fabric from
fashion houses. Designers such as Blune and
Tassia Canellis' delicate jewelry are also
displayed. A fashion line for children uses the
same fabric as the adults'. A bonus: Shelves
with toys and decoration objects. What else
do you need?
50, rue Jean-Pierre-Timbaud (11th). M° Parmentier.
Phone: 09 53 59 96 42.

By Sophie

BAKKER MADE WITH LOVE
BALI GAMES
**At Bakker, children and moms' fashion
lines match.** They are made in Bali using
unique prints. Designer Valérie Bakker lives in
Indonesia and creates graphic motifs in a
vintage style. We run here for her shirts and
dresses made for little and big girls alike.
Charming!
30, rue des Petites-Écuries (10th). M° Château d'Eau,
Bonne Nouvelle. Phone: 09 81 86 06 60.
bakkermadewithlove-shop.com

V.I.P.
SERVICES

FOREIGN LANGUAGE BABY-SITTING, LICE-EXTERMINATING COMMANDO, PLACES THAT WILL MAKE YOUR LIFE EASIER

ALVEUS
SMART HELP

This tutoring start-up is for middle and high-school students. Classes are given by young engineering students who act as big brothers and sisters, helping children in groups of three or four. The children are welcomed in a "hive" open seven days a week, for two to four hours of weekly tutoring or unlimited access to work alone. Let's get to work!

25, rue Bréa (6th). M° Vavin, Notre-Dame-des-Champs.
Phone: 09 83 71 94 91.
11, rue Augereau (7th).
M° École Militaire.
alveus.club

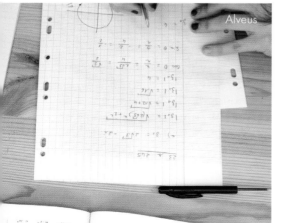

Alveus

MA SHARE ÉCOLE
VERY CLASSY

This amazing website allows parents whose kids attend the same elementary school to help each other out. Inside a "virtual classroom" created by parents of children in the same class, people help one another: school pick-ups, lunches, information on activities and homework, clothes exchange or sales. Everything is administrated and secured by the website creators.

mashareecole.com

WOMB Paris

BYEBYENITS
S.O.S. HEAD LICE

Have you tried every single treatment and failed? There is one solution left, both creative and practical: ByeByeNits.
This is the first anti lice center that offers to get rid of lice with a revolutionary procedure: a super-efficient machine that dries out the parasites and vacuums them without damaging the hair. A check-up seven days after the treatment is included in the 79€ plan.
Be gone, lice!
49, boulevard Richard-Lenoir (11th). M° Richard-Lenoir.
37, rue Ampère (17th). M° Wagram.
Phone: 01 53 81 66 59. byebyenits.com

WOMB PARIS
GREAT AND BEAUTIFUL
Are you looking for childcare items that are as beautiful as they are useful?
Go to this place, which offers a large array of services and parent-children workshops: baby massages, birthday planning, yoga classes, concierge.
93, rue Réaumur (2nd). M° Sentier.
Phone: 01 42 36 06 77.
wombconcept.com

SPEAKING-AGENCY
LANGUAGE TUITION
Everyone knows that the best way to learn a new language is complete and early-age immersion. Speaking-Agency connects you with bilingual nannies and baby-sitters who learned language tuition with a psycholinguist. Many different services are offered for all ages: activities, games, workshops or simple day-care.
33, boulevard Saint-Martin (3rd).
M° Strasbourg Saint-Denis, République.
Phone: 01 83 95 41 74.
speaking-agency.com

1 2 3 ciseaux

1 2 3 CISEAUX
A CLEAN CUT
This hairdressing establishment, with its custom-made children's seats, TV screens with kids' programs and a game room with duck fishing, books and video games for the older ones , is a favorite among children. From 20 to 27€ for a cut, depending on the age.
6, rue Dupont-des-Loges (7th).
M° École Militaire, RER Pont de l'Alma.
Phone: 01 53 59 94 52.
4, rue Papillon (9th). M° Poissonnière, Cadet.
Phone: 01 42 46 76 81.
10, boulevard de Courcelles (17th). M° Villiers.
Phone: 01 42 12 03 60.
123ciseaux.com

LITTLE **ART**
SMART AWAKENING
ACTIVITIES

Philharmonie de Paris

FONDATION
JÉRÔME SEYDOUX-PATHÉ
WELL THOUGHT OUT

The Fondation Jérôme Seydoux-Pathé organizes a journey through the history of cinema in a workshop for small movie lovers every Wednesday afternoon. "Le Petit Cinématographe" introduces them to the magic lantern process and to silent movies with, to top it all off, a participatory movie concert! Extra screenings with a themed program are scheduled during school breaks.
73, avenue des Gobelins (13th).
M° Gobelins, Place d'Italie.
Phone: 01 83 79 18 96.
fondation-jeromeseydoux-pathe.com

Centquatre

CENTQUATRE
WELL PLAYED

At 104, introductions to art start as young as six months old! La Maison des Petits welcomes infants (up to four years old) and parents for complicit playtime in its elegant decor by Matali Crasset. This friendly place was thought up based on the Maison Verte Dolto model. Little ones are also allowed "Toutes Petites Visites" (very small visits) of exhibitions where they can touch the artworks. The "Petits Chantiers" (small construction sites) allows them to build and destroy, while the "Rencontres Joyeuses" (joyful encounters) are readings of children's books.
5, rue Curial (19th). M° Riquet. Phone: 01 53 35 50 00.
104.fr

LITTLE VILLETTE
WELL CONNECTED
There is a paradise for children under twelve in Paris. Between porte de Pantin and porte de la Villette, this place is made up of different sites: the Cité des sciences at la Géode, outdoor play areas in the parc de la Villette and Little Villette, where children can access workshops (for a fee), and a reading room, circus room and Lego room freely. Kids will have fun and grow here, even when it is raining.

211, avenue Jean Jaurès (19ᵗʰ). M° Porte de Pantin.
Phone: 01 40 03 75 75.
lavillette.com

PHILHARMONIE DE PARIS
I HEAR YOU
The Philharmonie is not merely for adults. This musical palace has a rich program for children and teens: movie concerts with related workshops, fun visits of current exhibitions, musical awakening for babies under three months, thematic introductions to instruments, participatory concerts where entire families can prepare for the program. Music, everywhere!

211, avenue Jean-Jaurès (19ᵗʰ).
M° Porte de Pantin.
Phone: 01 44 84 44 84.
philharmoniedeparis.fr

CENTRE POMPIDOU
INSPIRED
Children are not forgotten at Centre Pompidou, where contemporary art is adapted for them. La Galerie des enfants is a temporary exhibition platform where children can let their imagination wander while immersing themselves in the world of a guest artist: take pictures with street artist JR, imagine cardboard constructions à la Kawamata. Great ideas!

Place Georges-Pompidou (4ᵗʰ).
M° Rambuteau, Hôtel de Ville.
Phone: 01 44 78 15 78.
centrepompidou.fr

Little Villette

MUSÉE EN HERBE
All year long, the Musée en herbe bends over backward for children. From three years old, kids are offered guided visits to current exhibitions, workshops related thematically to the exhibition. Here are many ideas to awaken our little ones' minds.
23, rue de L'Arbre-Sec (1ˢᵗ). M° Louvre-Rivoli.
Phone: 01 40 67 97 66. museeenherbe.com.

INDEX

FRIENDS OF ELLE

Serge Bensimon (p. 41)
Addresses on bensimon.com

Aurélie Bidermann (p. 67)
55 bis, rue des Saints-Pères
(6th). Phone: 01 45 48 43 14.
aureliebidermann.com

Vanessa Bruno (p. 139)
100, rue Vieille du Temple
(3rd). Phone: 01 42 77 19 41.
12, rue de Castiglione (1st).
Phone: 01 42 61 44 60.
25, rue Saint Sulpice (6th).
Phone: 01 43 54 41 04.
vanessabruno.fr

Hélène Darroze (p. 20)
4, rue d'Assas (6th).
Phone: 01 42 22 00 11.
helenedarroze.com

Myriam De Loor (p. 117)
Petit Pan
37, rue François Mirron (4th).
Phone: 01 42 74 57 16.
Addresses on petitpan.com

Ines de la Fressange (p. 42)
Ines de la Fressange Paris
24, rue de Grenelle (7th).
Phone: 01 45 48 19 06.
inesdelafressange.fr

Valérie Gerbi (p. 119)
Merci
111, boulevard
Beaumarchais (3rd).
Phone: 01 42 77 00 33.
merci-merci.com

Camille Goutal (p. 93)
Maison Annick Goutal
Addresses on
annickgoutal.com

Pierre Hermé (p. 102)
72, rue Bonaparte (6th).
Phone: 01 43 54 47 77.
Addresses on
pierreherme.com

Aliza Jabès (p. 171)
Nuxe
Addresses on nuxe.com

Juliette Lévy (p. 85)
Oh My Cream !
3, rue de Tournon (6th).
Phone: 01 43 54 80 83.
4, rue des Abbesses (18th).
Phone: 09 86 24 36 51.
ohmycream.com

Isabel Marant (p. 163)
47, rue de Saintonge (3rd).
Phone: 01 42 78 19 24.
1, rue Jacob (6th).
Phone: 01 43 26 04 12.
16, rue de Charonne (11th).
Phone: 01 49 29 71 55.
151, avenue Victor
Hugo (16th).
Phone: 01 47 04 99 95.
isabelmarant.com

Christophe Michalak
(p. 147)
16, rue de la Verrerie (10th).
Phone: 01 40 27 90 13.
60, rue du Faubourg-
Poissonnière (10th).
Phone: 01 42 46 10 45.
christophemichalak.com

Martine de Richeville
(p. 143)
13, boulevard
Malesherbes (8th).
20, avenue Bosquet (7th).
Phone: 01 44 94 09 38.
martinedericheville.com

Anne-Sophie Pic
(p. 109)
La Dame de Pic
20, rue du Louvre (1st).
Phone: 01 42 60 40 40.
anne-sophie-pic.com

Véronique Piedeleu
(p. 101)
Caravane
6, rue Pavée (4th).
Phone: 01 44 61 04 20.
9, rue Jacob (6th).
Phone: 01 53 10 08 86.
19, rue Saint-Nicolas (12th).
Phone: 01 53 02 96 96.
22, rue Saint-Nicolas (12th).
Phone: 01 53 17 18 55.
caravane.fr

Delphine Plisson (p. 81)
La Maison Plisson
93, boulevard
Beaumarchais (3rd).
Phone: 01 71 18 19 09.
lamaisonplisson.com

Sigolène Prébois (p. 74)
Tsé & Tsé associées
7, rue Saint-Roch (1st).
Phone: 01 42 61 90 26.
Addresses on tse-tse.com

Sarah (p. 145)
Colette
213, rue Saint-Honoré (1st).
Phone: 01 55 35 33 90.
colette.fr

Vanessa Seward (p. 15)
10, rue d'Alger (1st).
Phone: 01 85 65 88 89.
7, boulevard des Filles
du Calvaire (3rd).
Phone: 01 70 36 06 11.
vanessaseward.com

Morgane Sezalory
Sézane (p. 137)
1, rue Saint-Fiacre (2nd).
sezane.com

Marie-Hélène de Taillac
(p. 115)
8, rue de Tournon (6th).
Phone: 01 44 27 07 07.
mariehelenedetaillac.com

CREDITS

All images have been graciously provided by the press officers of the boutiques, restaurants, bars, studios, hotels, etc. mentioned in this guide. We thank them warmly.

ELLE

SUPERVISED BY
Anne-Cécile SARFATI
assisted by Delphine LAPEYRÈRE

AUTHORS
Camille GIRETTE
Sabine ROCHE

ILLUSTRATOR
Soledad

WRITER-EDITOR
Alexandre MOUAWAD

ARTISTIC DIRECTION ELLE
Germain CHAUVEAU, Creative Director
Sheeno, Art Director

**ORIGINAL IDEA AND BOOKSHOPS
DIVERSIFICATION PROJECT COORDINATOR**
Anne-Françoise BÉDHET
assisted by Charlotte POUHET

EDITOR-IN-CHIEF
Françoise-Marie SANTUCCI

CEO ELLE FRANCE AND INTERNATIONAL
Constance BENQUÉ

DEPUTY MANAGING DIRECTOR
Flore SEGALEN

ASSOCIATED PUBLISHERS
Inma BÉVAN-RAMIREZ
Anne-Marie LABINY

CEO – ELLE INTERNATIONAL MEDIA LICENSES
François CORUZZI

AKNOWLEDGMENTS

THE AUTHORS THANK

Valia BREITEMBRUCH, Nathalie ELBAZ-FORISSIER, Caroline DE FAYET, Sandrine FURET, Danièle GERKENS, Delphine LAPEYRÈRE,
Fanny PLATEAU, Catherine ROIG, Isabelle SANSONETTI, Anne-Cécile SARFATI, Stéphanie SEMEDO, Capucine WEIL.

CAMILLE THANKS

Guirec, Gabin, Hugo, Aurélie, Oriane, Delphine, Nadja, Émeline, Catherine, Laurent, Édouard, Marie-Hélène,
Dominique, Capucine, Prune, Ségolène, Gatien, Gaëlle.

SABINE THANKS

Pascal, Phany, Nicole, Michèle, Olivier, Diego.

The ELLE team extends warm thanks to all their collaborators. But also, and most of all,
to their loyal readers that have been with them for over seventy years,
from mother to daughter and across generations.

ÉDITIONS DU CHÊNE

CEO
Fabienne Kriegel

EDITORIAL MANAGER
Valérie Tognali, assited by Sandrine Rosenberg

EDITOR
Laurence Basset

ART DIRECTOR
Sabine Houplain, assisted by Élodie Palumbo and Julie Delzant

GRAPHIC DESIGN
NWB Studio

ENGLISH TRANSLATION
Justine Granjard

PROOFREADING
Theresa Bebbington for Cillero & de Motta

ENGLISH LAYOUT
Vincent Lanceau

PHOTOGRAVURE :
APS Chromostyle

ELLE™ is used by Éditions du Chêne under license from HACHETTE FILIPACCHI PRESSE SA.
Published by Éditions du Chêne (58 rue Jean Bleuzen, CS 70007, 92178 Vanves Cedex)
Printed in Spain by Estella Graficas
Copyright registration: April 2017
ISBN 978-2-81231-635-7
31/2630/8-01